Unit - 1

ACCOUNTING PROCESS AND PRINCIPLES, FINANCIAL, COST AND MANAGEMENT ACCOUNTING

Unit Structure:

1.0   OBJECTIVES

After studying the unit the students will be able to:
- Understand the meaning of Accounting.
- Explain the Accounting Principles and Concepts.
- Know the Process of Accounting.
- Understand and explain the process of Accounting.

1.1   INTRODUCTION

Every person performs some kind of economic activity. A worker daily works and get wages and he spends to buy goods, cloths and some part of earnings saves for future. A business man purchases goods and sales it. He incurred various expenses like salaries, rent etc. A partner in firm contributes towards capital in the firm which carries on business may be trading in goods. Similarly companies, Governments are also carries on some financial activities. All are carrying some kind of economic activities. Such economic activities are performed through transactions and / or events. Thus the business transactions include purchase, sale of goods, rendering various services, receipts and payments for such transactions.

1

In a business concerns the transactions are numerous. The details of all transactions cannot be remembered by the business man. Therefore it is necessary to keep written records of all such transactions. The records of written transaction will help business to settle disputes and also possible to provide valuable information to the owner of business. Book-keeping disciple has been developed to serve this purpose. The aim of Book-keeping is to provide the information needed by the businessmen and also it helps him to take decisions.

1.2 MEANING OF ACCOUNTING

The American Institute of Certified Public Accounts (AICPA) defined Accounting as "Accountancy is the art of recording classifying and summarizing in a significant manner and in terms of money transactions and events which are in part of at least a financial characters and interpreting the result there of".

Again in 1966, AICPA defines Accounting as "The process of identifying, measuring and communicating economic information to permit; informed judgement and decisions by the uses of accounts".

Thus accounting may be defined as the process of recording, classifying, summarizing, analysing and interpreting the financial transactions and communicating the results. There of to the persons interested in such information.

The utility of accounting information is greatly increased when it is compiled in a systematic manner and financial statements are prepared at periodic intervals.

There is difference between the terms "Book keeping" and "Accounting". Book keeping is merely concerned with orderly record keeping and recording business transactions and financial Accounting is border in scope than book keeping. Accounting involves analysis and judgements at different stages such as recording of transactions, classification, summarization and interpretation.

1.3 ACCOUNTING PRINCIPLES

The basis aims of book-keeping and accountancy are to record the business transactions and events in a summarised form. Transactions are recorded in chronological order in proper books of accountsbook-keeping. Accountancy and science based or fundamental truth and rules or conducts or procedures which are universally accepted. These rules of conducts to record business transactions are called accounting principles. These principles are developed over long period of time.

The classification of accounting principles is as under:

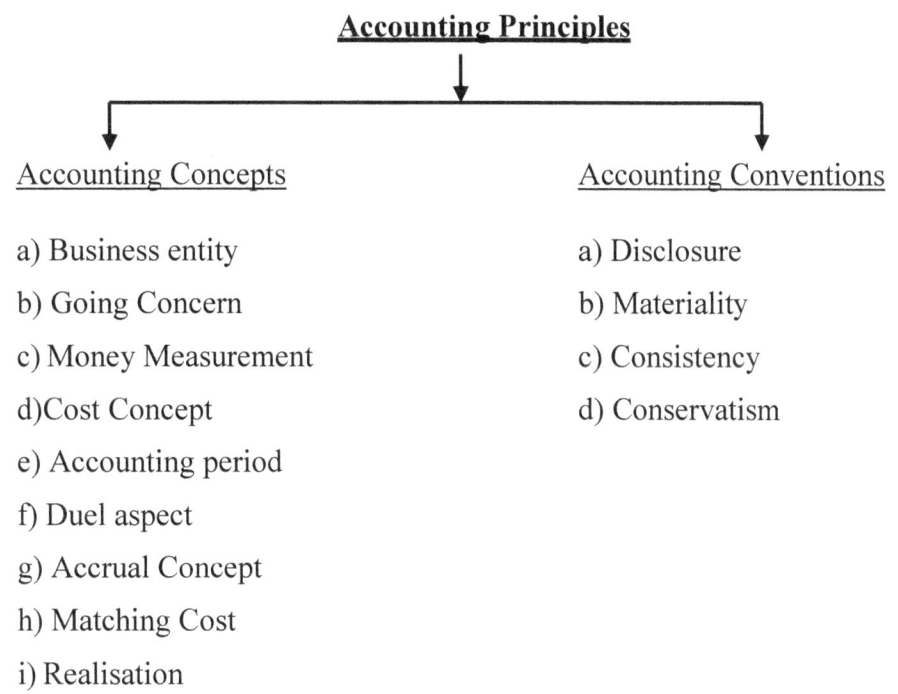

Accounting Principles

Accounting Concepts	Accounting Conventions
a) Business entity	a) Disclosure
b) Going Concern	b) Materiality
c) Money Measurement	c) Consistency
d)Cost Concept	d) Conservatism
e) Accounting period	
f) Duel aspect	
g) Accrual Concept	
h) Matching Cost	
i) Realisation	

1.3.1 Accounting Concepts:

Concepts mean a general idea which conveys certain meaning. Accounting concepts may be considered as basis assumption or conditions on which the science of accounting is based. Concepts are based on logical consideration. Accounts and Financial statements are always interpreted in light of concepts which govern accounting method.

Different accounting concepts are discussed as follows:

a. **Business Entity Concepts**

According to Entity concept, business is treated as a unit of entity form separate from its Owner, Creditors and Management etc. Accounts are kept for business entity as distinguished form a person associated with it. All business transactions are recorded in the books of Accounts from the point of view of business only. Every type of business organisation is treated as separate Accounting entity.

The failure to recognise the business as separate accounting entity would make it extremely difficult to evaluate the performance of business alone.

The overall effect of adopting this concept is –

1) Only the business transactions are reported and not the personal transactions of the owners.

2) Profit is the property of business unless distributed to the owners.

3) The personal assets of the owners are not considered while recording and reporting the assets of the business entity.

b. Going Concern

Business transactions are recorded on the assumption that the business will continue for a long time. There is neither the intention nor the necessity to liquate the particular business in near future. Therefore, it would be able to meet its contractual obligation and use its resources according to the plans and predetermined goals. Therefore, Fixed Assets are recorded at cost and depreciation is calculated on cost / written down value. Similarly prepaid expenses are treated as Assets on the presumption that the business will continue and these expenses will be utilized in future.

When an enterprise liquidates a branch or one division or one segment of its business, the ability of the enterprise to continue as a going concern is not imparted.

In case of enterprise going to liquidate or become insolvent. Then the enterprise cannot be considered as a going concern.

c. Money Measurement Concept

A unit of exchange and measurement is necessary to account for business transaction in a uniform manner. Money is common denominator in terms of which the exchange ability of goods and services are measured. Only such transactions and events as can be interpreted in terms of money are recorded.

Non monetary events like public political contract, location of business; certain disputes, efficient Sales Force etc. can not be recorded in the books of Accounts even through these have great effects.

However, a unit of money measurement over period of time has its own drawbacks. Money has time value, which can not be considered. Time value of money is affected seriously by economic differences etc. System of accountancy treats all units of money same irrespective of time of original and settlement of it say after two years. It will be the same amount. However value of Money true sense will be less. This is a great drawback. This leads to the introduction of inflation accounts.

d. Cost Concepts

According to cost concept the various assets acquired by enterprise should be recorded on the basis of actual cost incurred. The cost concept does not mean that the basis for all subsequent accounting for the assets. As per cost concept Fixed Assets are shown at cost less depreciation charged from year to year. It may be noted that if nothing has been paid for acquiring something it would not be shown/recorded in the books of accounts maintain.

Financial statement based on historical cost may not be much relevant for investors and other users because they are more interested in knowing what the business actually worth today rather than the original cost.

e. Accounting Period Concept

It is customary that the life of the business is divided into appropriate parts or segments of analysing the results shown by the business. Each part divided is known as an accounting period. It is an internal of time at end of which the income statement and balance sheet are prepared. Normally the accounting period consists of twelve months.

f. Duel Aspect Concept

This concept based on double Entry book-keeping which means that Accounting system is set up in such a way that a record is made of the two aspects of each transaction that affects the record. The recognition of the two aspects of every transaction is known as duel aspects concept. Modern Financial Accounting considers both aspects of every transaction.

One entry consists of debit to one or more accounts and another effect consist of credit to some other one or more accounts. However, the total amount debited is always equal to the total amount credited. Therefore at any point of time total assets of a business are equal to its total liabilities. Liabilities to outsider are known as liabilities, liabilities to the owner are referred to as capital.

Assets = Liabilities + Capital

Therefore, Capital = Assets – Liabilities

Assets referred to valuable things owned by the business, Capital refers to the owner"s contribution to the business.

g. Accrual Concept

This accounting concept states that revenue is recognised when they are earned and when they are not received similarly, cost are recognised as and when they are incurred and not when they are paid. This concept implies that the income should be measured as difference between revenues and expenses rather that the difference between cash received and disbursements. Therefore certain adjustments are required while preparing Final Accounts. In case of revenue accounts; prepaid expenses, out standing expenses, Income received in advance / Receivable are adjusted. These adjustments have their impact on both the income statement and the Balance sheet.

h. Matching Cost Concept

This concept is based on accounting period concept for determining accurate profit / Income has to compare the revenues of the business with the cost that is incurred to earn that revenue. The term "Matching" means appropriate association of related revenues and expenses. According to this concept adjustments should be made for all outstanding expenses, income receivable, prepaid expenses, Income received in advance, depreciation etc. While preparing final accounts at the end of accounting period.

i. Realisation Concept

This accounting concept explains that sell is supposed to be completed only when ownership of goods are passed on from the seller to the buyer. Income is considered to be earned on the date when sales take place. No profit is supposed to accrue on the acquisition of any thing, however, income earned / realised will be earn only when goods are sold at a profit. Therefore closing stock is valued at cost or market price whichever is less. It prevents business Firms from inflecting their profits by recording income that is expected in future.

1.3.2 Accounting Conventions:

The term „Convention" denotes customs or traditions or practice based on general agreement between the accounting bodies which guide the accountant while preparing the financial statements.

a. Disclosure

According to convention of full disclosure, accounting must disclose all the material facts and informations so that interested parties after reading such accounting report can get a clear view of the state of affairs of the business. All information which are of material interest to proprietors, creditors and investors should be disclosed in accounting statement.

The Companies Act makes various provisions for disclosure of essential information that their is no chance of any material information being left out.

b. Materiality

The term material means "relative importance", Accounting to the convention of materiality; account should report only what is material and ignore insignificant details while the preparing the final accounts. Materiality will differ or changed with nature, size and tradition of the business. What is material for one enterprise may be immaterial for another enterprise. This is because otherwise accounting will unnecessarily be overburdened with minute details. It is not possible to lay down any fixed standard by which Materiality can be judged. The decision is to be made by the accountant or the Auditor based on their professional experience.

c. Consistency

This accounting convention state that ones a particular accounting practice, method or policy is adopted to prepare accounts, statements and Reports. It should be continued for years together and should not charge unless it is forced to change it. Accounting practices should remain the same from one year to another. The results of different years will be comparable only when accounting rules are continuously adhered to from years to years i.e. Valuation of stock in trade, method of depreciation, treatment of approval sale etc. Since methods of accounting consistence the financial statements are reliable to the people who use it.

d. Conservatism

Financial Statements are usually drawn up on a conservative basis. Their are two principles which stem directly from conservatism.

a) The accountant should not anticipate income and should provide all possible losses, and

b) Faced with the choice between two methods of valuing an asset the accountant should choose a method which leads to the lesser value.

It is also called "Principles of prudence". Therefore, provision for bad and doubtful debts is also permitted and made every year. Accounting convention must be followed continuously. If not followed continuously it would result into understatement of incomes, assets and overstatement of liabilities and provisions and expenses.

1.4   BRANCHES OF ACCOUNTING

Accounting has forms of branches as under

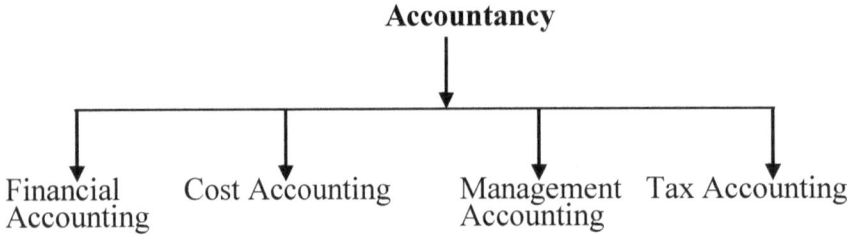

1.4.1   Financial Accounting

It is concerned with record keeping directed towards the preparation of Trial balance, profit and loss account and balance sheet.

1.4.2   Cost Accounting

Cost Accounting is the process of accounting for costs. It shows classification and analysis of cost on the basis of functions process, products etc. It also deals with cost computation, cost saving, cost reduction etc. In cost accounting cost per unit of output produced or services rendered is ascertained. It helps management in the control of cost of output or services rendered.

1.4.3   Management Accounting

It deals with the processing of data sentenced in financial accounting and cost accounting for managerial decision making. It also deals with application of managerial economic concepts for decision making for the efficient running of the business and thus in maximising profits.

1.4.4   Tax Accounting

This branch of accounting is becoming important because of complex tax laws governing income-tax, Excise duty, value added tax etc. Tax planning is now a days is very important as well to save tax, Account for tax deducted at sources, payment of advance tax, Filing of various tax returns in time as well as taking Cenvat credit for various taxes whenever is available.

1.5   ACCOUNTING PROCESS

The process of accounting involves recording classifying and summarizing of past events and transactions of financial nature, with a view to enabling the user of accounts to interpret the resulting summary.

The utility of accounting information is greatly increased when it is complied in a systematic manner and financial statements prepared at periodic intervals.

The Accounting Process

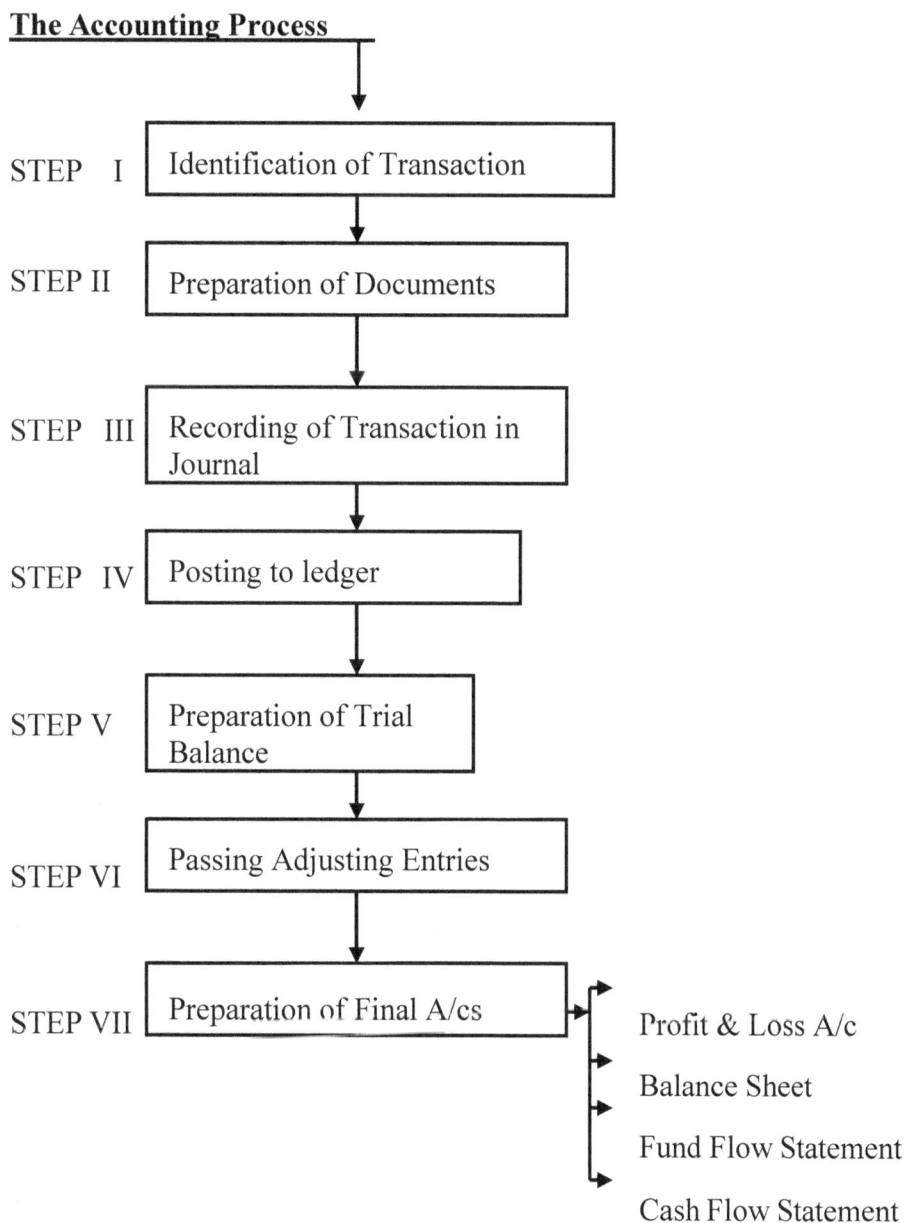

Note: As final Accounts are separately explains in subsequent chapter, here only fund flows & cash flows statements are explained.

CHECK YOUR PROGRESS

- Define the following terms:
  1. Cost Concept
  2. Business entity concept
  3. Going concern concept
  4. Duel aspect concept
- Explain the following Accounting conventions:
  1. Disclosure
  2. Consistency
- Draw the chart showing Accounting Process.

1.6 FUND FLOW STATEMENT

The fund flow statement reflects movement of fund during particular period i.e. movement of working capital. Funds means working capital and not only cash/Bank balances. Sources consider of the transactions that increases net working capital and their applications consist of transactions that decrease working capital.

Specimen of funds flow statement

Funds flow statement for the year ended.....

Sources		Applications	
Issue of Share Capital	x	Redemption of preference shares	x
Issue of Debentures	x	Redemption Debentures	x
Sale of Fixed Assets	x	Repayment of loan Term loans	x
Sale of Investments	x	Purchased of Fixed Assets	x
Long term Loans	x	Purchased of Investment	x
Decrease in working capital	x	Dividend paid	x
Funds from operations (Cash Trading Profit)	x	Income Tax paid	x
		Buy-Back of Equity shares	x
		Increase in working capital	x
	xx		**xx**

In short fund flows statement indicates various sources of working capital and its applications.

1.7   CASH FLOW STATEMENT

Cash flow statement shows inflows and outflows of cash/ cash equivalent. It is prepared as per A.S-3.

As per A.S-3, the cash flow statement should report cash flows during the period classified as operating, Investing and financing activities.

Activities that do not require use of cash / cash equivalents should be excluded from a cash flow statement. e.g. Issue of Bonus shares conversion of Debentures into new Debentures / Shares.

Cash flow statement can be prepared by Direct method or Indirect method.

Under direct method, major classes of gross cash receipts and gross cash payments are obtained for showing it in funds from operations.

Indirect method, cash flow operating activities is calculated by adjusting net profit. Net profit is adjusted, with non cash transaction such as depreciation, Goodwill w/off etc, result figure indicates cash operating profit, which further adjusted with net increases / decreases in current Assets / Current liabilities. The final amount resulted indicates cash flows operating activities.

Proforma of cash flow statement As per A.S-3 (Indirect Method)

Cash Flow statement for the year ended ....

	Rs.	Rs.
I) **Cash flows from operating Activities**		
Net profit before taxations	x	
Add: Adjustment for		
Depreciation, Goodwill w/off	x	
Loss on sale of fixed Assets / Investment	x	
Interest / Dividend Income	x	
Operating profit before working capital changes	xx	
Increases in working capital	(x)	
Decreases in working capital	x	
Cash generated from operations	x	
Cash Income Tax paid	(x)	
Net cash from operating activities		x

II)	**Cash flows from Investing Activities**		
	Sale of Fixed Assets / Investment	x	
	Interest / Dividend received	x	
	Purchased of fixed assets / Investment	(x)	
	Net cash flow from investing activities		x
III)	**Cash flows from financing Activities**		
	Proceeds from Issurance of share capital	x	
	Proceeds from Issurance of Debentures	x	
	Proceeds from long term loans Repayment of	x	
	long term loans Redemption of Pref. Shares /	(x)	
	Debenture Interest / Dividend paid	(x)	
	Net cash used in financing activities	(x)	
	Net increases or decreases in cash / cash equivalents		x
	Add: Cash/ cash equivalents at the beginning of the period.		xx
			x
	Cash / cash equivalent at the end of period.		
			xx

1.8 DISTINCTION BETWEEN FUNDS FLOW STATEMENT AND CASH FLOW STATEMENT

Both the above statement are used in analysis of past performance of the business firm.

	Fund Flow Statement		**Cash Flow Statement**
1.	It is based on accrued accounting system	1.	All cash and cash equivalents are taken into consideration
2.	It analyses the sources & application in Long term funds affecting working capital	2.	Cash flows statements considers only the transactions affecting increases or decreases in current assets or / and current liabilities.
3.	It is more useful in Long-run planning	3.	It help form in identifying the current liquidity problems.
4.	It is broader concepts, considering short term / long term funds into accounts in analysis.	4.	It only deals with current assets/ current liabilities shown in Balance sheet.

5.	It tallies the funds generated from various sources with various uses to which they are put.	5.	It shows in increases or decreases in cash/ cash equivalent during the period, which tallies with difference inopening / closing cash / Bank balances.
6.	It shows the funds generated and applied as regards long term assets & liabilities.	6.	It shows the cash flows from operating, financing and investing activities.

1.9   EXERCISES :

1. Are the accounting concepts and conventions necessary?

2. Explain meaning of:

    a) Accounting concepts

    b) Accounting conventions c)

    Accounting principles

3. Explain accounting conventions of:

    a) Conservatism

    b) Consistency

    c) Disclosure

    d) Materiality

4. Define and explain:

    a) Concept of entity

    b) Concept of continuity

    c) Cost concept

    d) Cost attach concept

    e) Periodic matching of costs and revenues

5. Explain different branches of Accounting.

□□□□

Unit - 2

ELEMENT OF BOOK-KEEPING, JOURNAL, CASH AND BANK BOOK-I

Unit Structure:

2.0 Objectives
2.1 Meaning of Book-keeping
2.2 Objective of Book-keeping
2.3 Utility of Book-keeping
2.4 Book-keeping and Accountancy
2.5 Accounting system
2.6 Account
2.7 Classification of Accounts
2.8 Rules of Debit & Credit
2.9 Books of Accounts
2.10 A conceptual framework of financial accounting
2.11 Journal
2.12 Solved Problems
2.13 Exercises

2.0 OBJECTIVES

After studying the unit the students will be able to:
- Know the Meaning, utility and objectives of Book keeping.
- Explain the Accounting system.
- Know the Classification of Accounts.
- Understand the rules of Debit and Credit.
- Explain the Meaning and Utility of Journal.
- Journalise the Business transactions.

2.1 MEANING OF BOOK-KEEPING

The oxford dictionary defines Book-keeping as "The activities of keeping records of financial dealings".

J.R. Batiboi defines book-keeping as, "Book-keeping is the art of recording business dealings in set of Books".

R.N. Carter defines book-keeping as "The science and art of correctly recording in the books of accounts. All those business transactions and events inset of books, as and when such transactions take place. It is a systematic recording in terms of money in set of books."

2.2   OBJECTIVES OF BOOK-KEEPING

The main objectives of Book-keeping are given below:

1. To maintain the permanant records of the business transactions.

2. To ascertain the profit earned or loss suffered during accounting period.

3. To know various business Assets and liabilities apart from the above main objectives.

4. To know amount due to businessman from his customers.

5. To know amount payable to Suppliers.

6. To know various taxes and duties payable to government.

7. To defect and prevent errors and frauds committed by employees and other person.

8. To provide valuable informations for taking for taking various decisions.

9. To take decision on significant business matters.

10. To compare and measure the optional efficiency of his business with other firm, companies in same type of Industry.

11. To review the progress of the business from year to year.

12. To maintain permanent record of all transactions of business for future reference.

13. To excise effective control on various expenses, incomes earned over business assets, business liabilities.

14. Other firms, Companies and within the firm compare current year with previous years. Such comparison is known as infra-firm comparison.

2.3   UTILITY OF BOOK- KEEPING

Utility means usefulness. The utilities to different persons and entities are as under:

1) Businessman:

The owner who invest his money and assets into his business. He must know the profitabilities, financial stability. The owner can take various decisions on the basis of the valuable information obtained from books of accounts.

2) **Evidence:**

Books of Accounts can be produced as evidence in a court of law in case of disputes.

3) Book-keeping ensures proper calculation of Income Tax, Sales Tax, VAT and other tax liabilities.

4) **Lenders:**

On the basis of information from books, it is possible to obtain additional finance for business and working capital. On the basis of such information, lender can be provided any additional information along with various financial statements.

5) **Trade Union:**

On the basis of financial statement Trade union can insist like in Wages, Bonus etc.

6) **Prospective Investors:**

Prospective Investor can take investment decision by studying financial statements.

7) **Comparative Study:**

Financial statement of business enterprise may be compared over a period of years inter firm and can be compared with two or more business enterprise in same type of Business over period of years. This is known as inter firm comparison. Such comparison helps businessman to judge profitabilities and efficient of his business.

2.4   BOOK- KEEPING AND ACCOUNTANCY

Book-keeping and Accounting they are differ from each other. Book-keeping is mainly concern with recording of financial data relating to business operations in a significant and orderly manner. It is mechanical and repetitive.

Accounting is a broader and more analytical subject. It includes the design of accounting system which book-keepers use to preparation of financial statement, audit, cost studies, Income tax, value added tax etc. Analysis and interpretation of accounting information for internal and external end users as on aid to making business decision. Book-keeping provides the basis of accounting.

2.5   ACCOUNTING SYSTEM

There are two accounting system of keeping records.

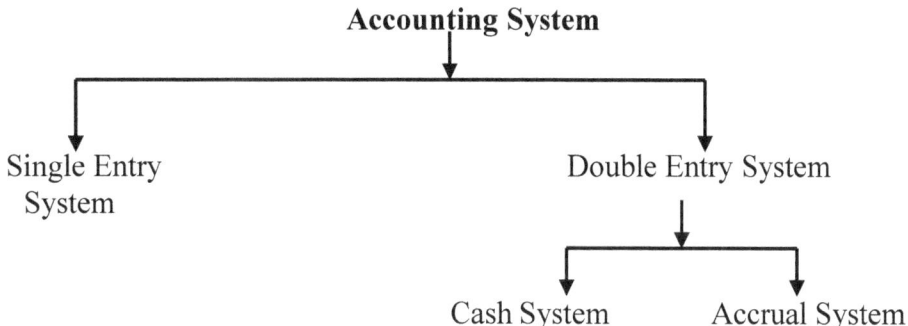

2.5.1 Single Entry System:

The single entry system appears to be time saving and economical but it is unscientific, having number of defects. Under single Entry system only few personal accounts are kept, as nothings; Expenses / Income accounts are totally ignored. This system is followed by sole proprietor, having total control on cash as well as on goods. However this system is not generally followed by any trader.

2.5.2 Double Entry System:

The Double entry system is based on scientific principle and is used universally by most of business organisations. This system recognises the fact that every transaction has two aspects and records both aspects of each and every transaction. Every business transaction involves exchange of equal values or benefits. Exchange means the act of giving or receiving one thing in return of the other thing or service or benefit. Thus every transaction has two aspects i.e. receiving and giving. The receiving aspect is also known as the incoming aspect (Debit) and going aspect is known as the outgoing aspect (credit).

Under double entry system books of accounts can be maintained by either cash basis or accrual basis.

- **Cash System of Accounting**

Under cash system of accounting entries are made only when cash is received or paid. No entry is made when amount is due for receipts or payments. Income is received is accounted irrespective of period for which relates. Similarly expenses are restricted to the actual payments made in cash, during the current period is immaterial whether the payments have been made for previous year or subsequent year.

The financial statement prepare under this system do not present a true and fair view of Income, operating results of enterprise. However it is suitable in following cases.

i) For very small business organisation.

ii) For individual to record his own transactions.

iii) For professionals like Doctors, Lawyers, Chartered Accountant etc.

In cash system financial statements are prepared on the basis of Receipts and payments accounts.

- **Accrual System of Accounts**

This is also known as mercantile system of accounts. Under this system business transactions are recorded as and when it take place irrespectful of amount / cash received or paid. Income earned as well as expenses incurred are recorded related to the Particular period. The following are the essential features of accrual basis.

a) Revenue is recognised on it is earned irrespective of whether cash is received or not.

b) Costs are matched against revenues on the basis of relevant time period to determined periodic income.

c) Costs which are not charged to income are carried forward. Any cost that lost its utility is written off as a loss.

2.6   ACCOUNT

An account is summarised record or statement of all transactions relating to a particular person or to a Assets or liability or income or expense.

According to Kohler"s Dictionary for accounts, An account has been defined as a formal record of a particular type of transaction expressed in money.

Each account is divided into two parts by the vertical line drawn in the middle.

Dr.   ....Account   Cr.

Date	Particulars	JF	Amount	Date	Particulars	JF	Amount

The left hand side is termed as Debit (Dr.) side and the right hand side is termed as credit (cr.) side.

In order to keep full record of all the transactions the business has to keep.

18

i) An account of each head of expenses or income earned by the business and

ii) An account of each property which belongs to the business and

iii) An account of each party with whom business deals.

2.7   CLASSIFICATION OF ACCOUNTS :

Accounts are classified into two classes:
- Personal Accounts
- Impersonal Accounts

Impersonal Accounts are further sub divided into
1. Real Accounts
2. Nominal Accounts
3. Valuation Accounts

Thus all accounts can be classified into Personal, Real and Nominal Accounts.

2.7.1   Personal Accounts:
These accounts show the transactions with customers, suppliers, Money lenders, the banks and the owner.
For example: Mohan"s A/c, Rajesh"s A/c, M/s XY and Co. Reliance Industries Ltd., Apna Bazar Co-operative Society Ltd., Mumbai University, Dena Bank etc.

2.7.2   Real Accounts:

Real accounts may be the following types.

a) Tangible real Accounts: These are accounts of such things which are tangible i.e. which can be seen touched or felt physically. Example: Land, Building, Furniture, Cash etc.

b) Intangible real Accounts: These accounts represent such things which cannot be touched, seen or felt physically.
Example: Goodwill, Trade marks, Patent right etc.
2.7.3   Nominal Accounts:
Nominal Accounts includes accounts of all expenses, losses, incomes and gains. Nominal Accounts represent only services or uses.
2.7.4   Valuation Accounts:

Valuation accounts are accounts open to adjust values of assets e.g. provision for Depreciation, Stock Reserve, Provision for doubtful debt A/c.

2.8   RULES OF DEBIT AND CREDIT :

The two sides of any account are arbitrarily distinguished. The left hand side of an Account is called Debit side and Right hand side is called the Credit side.

When entry on the left side is made it is called account is debited, and an Entry made on the right hand side of account is called account is credited.

An account is capable of receiving and giving values. When an account receives a value / benefit. It is debited and when it gives a value / benefit it is credited. Each business transactions affects at least two accounts. One account receives benefit of certain value, another account would give the benefit of the same value. The difference between the total debits and total credits in the accounts is considered as balance.

A) Personal Accounts

The personal Account which receives the benefit is debited, while the personal account which gives the benefit is credited. The fundamental rule of Debit and Credit regarding personal Account is Debit the Receiver And Credit the Giver

The rule means, if a person receives anything from the business, his account will be debited in the books of business, and if person gives anything to the business, his account will be credited.

Illustrations 1

Suppose Goods sold on credit to Sunil from the view point of business Sunil is a receiver because he receives goods and therefore Sunil"s Account will be debited.

Subsequently cash is received from Sunil. Mr. Sunil becomes a giver because he gives cash and hence his account will be credited.

B) Real Accounts

As a thing either comes in into business or goes out of business.

Debit-What Comes In
Credit-What Goes Out

Real account relates to things or property. Hence the above rule says if anything is coming into business, account of thing is to be debited and anything is going out of business account of that thing is to be credited.

In the Illustration goods are sold to Mr. Sunil on credit. Goods are going out of business and therefore "Goods A/c" is to be credited subsequently cash is received from Sunil. Cash is comes in therefore cash Account is to be debited.

C) Nominal Accounts

Being the accounts of losses and expenses or gains and incomes.

Debit Expenses and Losses
Credit Incomes and Gains.

Dr.	Nominal Accounts	Cr.
Payment of Salary, rent loss on sale of Assets. Bad Debts etc	Received Commission. Interest Discount etc.
Debit losses and expenses.	Credit Incomes and Gains

The accounts of expenses or losses of the business are to be debited where as the accounts of Incomes or profits are to be credited Exp. Paid salaries.

Here Salary is on expenditure of the business and therefore Salary account is to be debited.

In the transaction "Received Interest from A & Co" Interest is an Income of the business and hence Interest Account is to be credited.

Illustration. 2

State the names of the accounts to be debited or credited in the following transactions.

No.	Transactions	Name of accounts affected	Classification of account	Application of the rules	Answers
1.	Sujit Commenced business with cash	Sujit"s Capital A/c	Personal A/c	Credit the giver	Credit
		Cash A/c	Real A/c	Cash comes in Debit what comes in	Debit
2.	Purchased goods for cash	Goods A/c	Real A/c	Goods are comes in	Debit
		Cash A/c	Real A/c	Cash is goes out	Credit
3.	Sold goods on credit to Mr. Avinash	Avinash"s A/c	Personal A/c	Avinash is receiver	Debit
		Goods A/c	Real A/c	Goods are goes out	Credit
4.	Cash received from Mr. Avinash	Cash A/c	Real A/c	Cash comes In	Debit
		Avinash"s	Personal A/c	Avinash is	Credit
5.	Cash deposited into the Bank	Cash A/c	Real A/c	Cash goes out	credit
		Bank A/c	Personal A/c	Bank is receiver	Debit

2.9 BOOKS OF ACCOUNTS :

A business organisations maintains three types books of Accounts; namely,

Cash Book:

To record cash receipts and payments including receipts and Payments through Bank. A separate cash book is kept to record petty expenses.

Journal:

To record non cash transactions like credit sales, credit purchases, Sales Returns, Purchase Returns. These Books are called Subsidiary books.

Ledger:

Ledger contains a classified summary of all transactions recorded in cash book and journal. All personal, Real and Nominal Accounts are prepared into the ledger.

Few additional books of account may be maintained as per requirement of business organisation e.g. Stock Register, Members Register etc.

2.10 A CONCEPTUAL FRAMEWORK OF FINANCIAL ACCOUNTING :

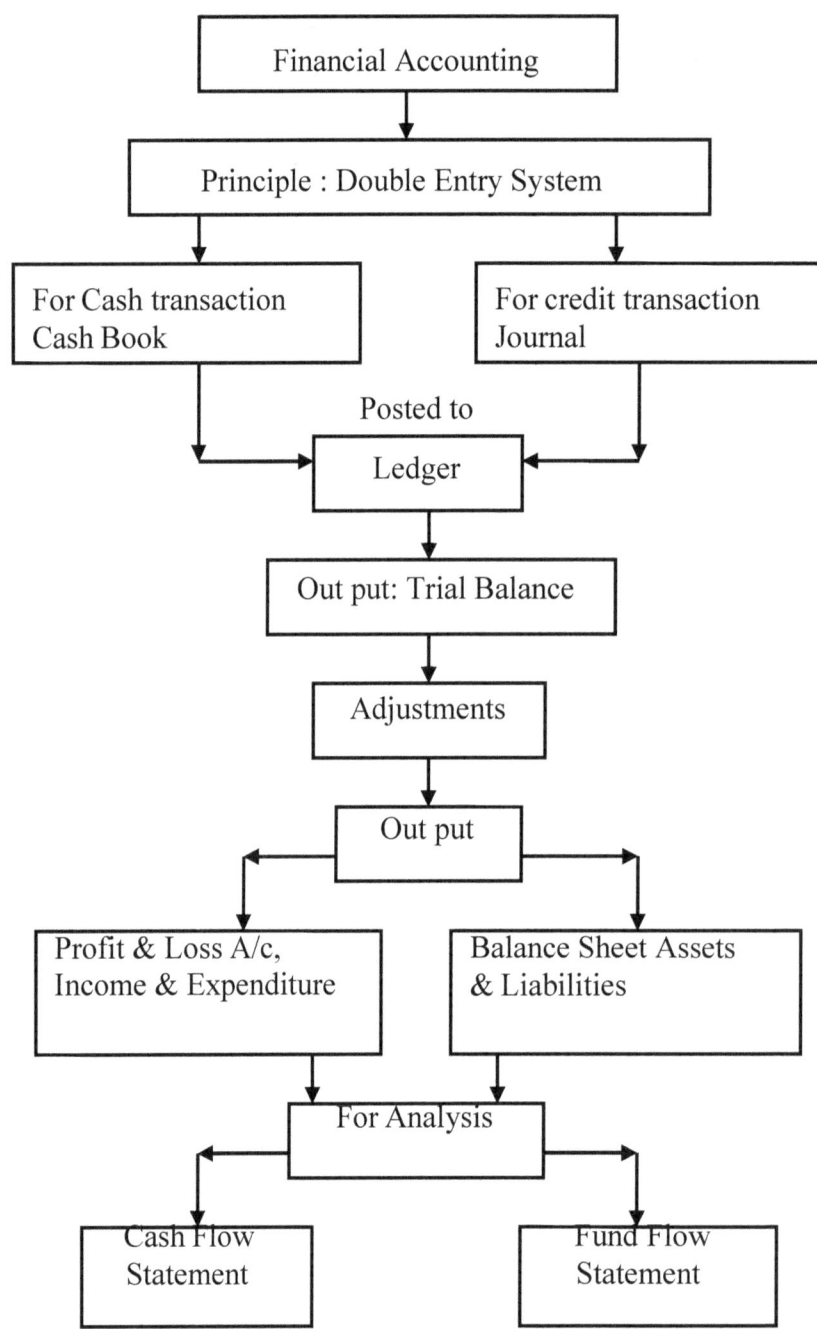

2.11 JOURNAL :

2.11.1 Meaning:

It is essential in a business to record each and every transaction immediately after it takes place. To record credit transaction a separate book, called „Journal" is maintain, Journal can be defined as, „a subsidiary book in which all day-to-day monetary transactions of business are recorded first as and when they take place in chronological order (i.e. date wise), in debit and credit form and in a systematic manner. Journal is also known as „Prime entry" or „Original entry" book. Because transactions are first entered in this book and then they are posted in the Ledger.

As Business transactions are numerous and large in size, the Journal may be split up into number of separate Journals to record particular type of transaction. These journal are known as the subsidiary books. Some of the subsidiary books are:

i) Purchase Book

ii) Purchase Return Book

iii) Sales Book

iv) Sales Return Book

v) Bills Receivable Book

vi) Bills Payable Book

vii) Journal Proper

2.11.2 Necessity or Utility of Journal

1. Direct recording of transactions in the ledger may result in committing errors and omissions and it would be difficult to correct them later on. Hence, Journal is necessary.

2. A complete record (i.e. Debit and credit aspects of each transaction) is available at one place.

3. As the transactions are recorded date wise, it facilitates quick and easy reference to any transaction, whenever necessary.

4. Narration to Journal entry explains the purpose of the entry and helps in understanding the transaction recorded.

5. Entries in the ledger can be made at leisure by the clerk concerned according to his convenience.

6. Cross checking between Journal and Ledger is facilitated to check the accuracy.

7. As the entries in the Journal are made from basic documents like invoices. Vouchers, receipts etc. The court considers the entries in the Journal as proof of transactions.

2.11.3 Specimen of Journal:

Date	Particulars	Voucher No.	LF	Dr. Amt. (Rs.)	Cr. Amt. (Rs.)

Journalising: The act of recording a transaction in the Journal in the form required is called Journalising.

2.11.4 How to Journalise the Transactions

1. First find out the two accounts involved in a transaction.

2. Ascertain the types of those accounts and then decide by applying rules of Debit and Credit as to which account is to be debited and which account is to be credited.

3. The name of the account is to be debited is to be written first under „Particulars" column. It is written close to the first margin line and the name of the account to be credited is to be proceeded by the word "To" and is to be written on the Second line.

4. The amount involved in the transactions is written under the "Dr" and "Cr" columns against the names of debit and credit accounts respectively.

5. A brief explanation of the entry is given in the bracket just below the entry. It is called "narration".

6. A line is drawn below each Journal Entry from first margin line to the second margin line to keep the entries of the transaction separate from one another.

7. Ledger folio (L.F.): It means page number in the ledger. The page on which the particular account is opened in the "Ledger" is stated under "L.F." column to facilite easy reference.

8. Date: The date of the transaction is written under the column "Date".

2.11.5 Debit note and Credit note:

Debit Note:

When goods are received from the supplier, the Supplier account is credited. When goods are returned from him the supplier account is debited, so in case of purchase returns a debit note is prepared. It should contain all the details of purchase returns. Generally a debit note will be made in duplicate, one copy will be sent to the customer and other will be kept as office copy.

Credit Note:

It is a statement sent by the seller to his customer intimating that, his account has been credited with the amount of goods return by him or any other allowances granted to him.

2.12 SOLVED PROBLEMS

Illustration 1

Journalise the following transactions in the books of "Ketan".
2009
Jan. 1 Purchased goods from Nalini on Credit Rs. 1000/-. Jan.
2 Sold goods to Mr. Sharma on credit Rs. 2,500/- Jan. 3
Purchased furniture for cash Rs. 10,000/-
Jan. 4 Received interest Rs. 800
Jan. 5 Paid salaries Rs. 3,500/-

After deciding the accounts to be debited and accounts to be credited the Journal Entries are passed as shown below.

In the Books of Ketan
Journal Entreis

Date	Particulars	L.F.	Dr. Rs.	Cr. Rs.
2009				
Jan.1	Purchases A/c .... .Dr. To Nalini"s A/c (Being goods purchased on credit from Nalini)		1,000	1,000
2	Mr. Sharma"s A/c ....Dr. To Sales A/c (Being goods sold on credit to Mr. Sharma)		2,500	2,500
3	Furniture A/c ....Dr. To Cash A/c (Being furniture purchased for Cash)		10,000	10,000

27

4	Cash A/c .... .Dr. To Interest A/c (Being interest received)			800	800
5	Salaries A/c ....Dr. To Cash A/c (Being Salaries paid)			3,500	3,500
		Total		**17,800**	**17,800**

Illustration 2

Journalise the following transactions in the books of Shri. More.

2009

Dec. 1 Shri More started business with cash Rs. 15000.

    2 Purchased goods from Mr. Singh Rs. 30,000

    3 Deposited cash into the Bank Rs. 4,000

    4 Sold goods to Mr. Gujar Rs. 2,500

    5 Purchased furniture of Rs. 2,500 from furniture and Co.

    6 Paid to Mr. Singh by cheque Rs. 1,000

    7 Received a cheque from Mr. Gujar Rs. 1,200

    8 Paid Interest Rs. 450

    9 Withdraw cash Rs. 3,000 for personal use

    10 Cheque received from Mr. Gujar Deposited into the Bank.

    11 Returned goods to Mr. Singh Rs. 500

    12 Received goods returned by Mr. Gujar Rs. 300

    13 Paid salary by cheque Rs. 4,000

    14 Received a cheque for rent Rs. 900. The cheque is deposited into the Bank.

    15 Withdraw cash Rs. 3,000 from Bank for office use.

    16 Returned Furniture of Rs. 400 to Furniture and company.

In the books of Shri. More.
Journal Entries

Date	Particulars	L.F.	Dr. Rs.	Cr. Rs.
2009				
Dec.1	Cash A/c . ... .Dr. To Capital A/c (Being started business with cash)		15,000	15,000
2	Purchases A/c ....Dr To Mr. Singh"s A/c (Being credit purchases from Mr. Singh)		30,000	30,000

28

3	Bank A/c ....Dr. To Cash A/c (Being Cash deposited in the bank)		4,000	4,000
4	Gujar''s A/c ....Dr. To Sales A/c (Being goods sold on credit to Mr. Gujar)		2,500	2,500
5	Furniture A/c ....Dr. To Furniture & Co. A/c (Being furniture purchased on credit)		2,500	2,500
6	Singh''s A/c ....Dr. To Bank A/c (Being issued a cheque to Mr. Singh)		1,000	1,000
7	Cash A/c .... Dr. To Mr. Gujar''s A/c (Being Cheque received from Mr. Gujar)		1,200	1,200
8	Interest A/c ....Dr. To Cash A/c (Being Interest paid)		450	450
9	Drawings A/c ....Dr. To Cash A/c (Being Mr. More withdraw cash for personal use)		3,000	3,000
10	Bank A/c ....Dr. To Cash A/c (Being cheque deposited into the Bank)		1,200	1,200
11	Mr. Singh''s A/c ....Dr. To Purchase Return A/c (Being Goods returned to Mr. Singh)		500	500
12	Sales Return A/c .... Dr. To Mr. Gujar''s A/c (Being Goods returned by Mr. Gujar)		300	300
13	Salaries A/c ....Dr. To Bank A/c (Being cheque issued for Salaries)		4,000	4,000

14	Bank A/c ....Dr. To Rent A/c (Being a cheque from the subtenant in payment of Rent and the cheque is deposited into the Bank)		900	900
15	Cash A/c ....Dr. To Bank A/c (Being cash withdrawn from Bank for office use)		3,000	3,000
16	Furniture and Co"s A/c .....Dr. To Furniture A/c (Being Furniture returned to Furniture and Co"s A/c)		400	400
	Total		**69,950**	**69,950**

The students will note that the total Debits is always equal to total of credits.

The entries in which there are more than one debit or more than one credit are called compound Entries.

2.13 EXERCISE

2.13.1 Theory Questions
1.   Explain term „Book Keeping.
2.   What is Account?
3.   Distinguish between:
   a) Book-keeping and Accountancy
   b) Personal Accounts and impersonal Accounts c) Real Accounts and Nominal Accounts
   d) Single Entry system and Double Entry system
   e) Cash system of Accounts and Accrual system of Accounts.
4.   Discuss the principles of debit and credit of Accounts.
5.   Explain Journal & its utility.
6.   "By sub-division of journal, there will be a division of labour". Explain.

2.13.2 Practical Problems

1) Journalise the following transactions in the books of Ram for the month of March 2010.

March 1 Ram commenced business with cash Rs. 60,000.

2 Purchased furniture for Rs. 5,000.

4 Purchased goods for cash Rs. 2,000.

7 Bought goods from M/s. Raj & Co. for Rs. 4,000.

10 Sold goods costing Rs. 3,000 on cash.

15 Purchased stationery for office use Rs. 1,000.

19 Received cash Rs. 1,250 from Mr. Ketan in full settlement of his account for Rs. 1,500.

20 Paid salaries by cheque Rs. 1,500.

25 Introduced additional capital Rs. 20,000.

27 Paid to Raj Rs. 3,250 in full settlement of Rs. 3,500

29 Sold goods for Rs. 15,000 to Mr. Dohi.

31 Deposited Rs. 3,000 into the Bank.

2) Journalise the following transactions in the books of Mr. Shiva for the month of April 2010.

April 1 Started business with cash Rs. 25,000/-

2 Purchased goods worth Rs. 10,000/-

4 Deposited cash Rs. 3,000 into the Bank.

6 Purchased goods of Rs. 6,000 from M/s. Raju Trading Company.

9 Sold goods to Mr. Ramesh for Rs. 3,000.

12 Paid to M/s. Raju Trading Company Rs. 3,000.

15 Received Rs. 1,000 from Mr. Ramesh.

20 Paid salaries Rs. 1,000/- and paid commission Rs. 1,600/- in cash.

25 Bought stationery for office use Rs. 300.

27 Withdrew Rs. 2,500 from business for personal use.

29 Withdrew Rs. 4,000 from bank for office use.

3) Journalise the following transactions in the journal of Mr. Anand for the month of February, 2010.

Feb 1 Borrowed from Bank @ 15% interest Rs. 20,000.

3 Purchased goods from Mr. Sam for Rs. 3,500.

4 Paid carriage and cartage Rs. 250

7 Sold goods on cash Rs. 3,000.

10 Paid Rs. 2,250 to Mr. Sam.

15 Purchased office furniture for Rs. 6,000.

18 Paid interest Rs. 450/- to Mr. Bank.

20 Paid salaries Rs. 6,000.

22 Cash sales Rs. 20,000.

26 Cash purchases Rs. 15,000

28 Paid Rs. 2,000 to Bank in part payment of loan.

Unit - 3
ELEMENT OF BOOK-KEEPING, JOURNAL, CASH AND BANK BOOK-II

Unit Structure:

3.0 Objectives
3.1 Cash Book
3.2 Cash Discounts
3.3 Petty Cash Book
3.4 Three Column Cash Book
3.5 Exercises

3.0   OBJECTIVES

After studying the unit the students will be able to:

- Know the Meaning of Cash book.

- Understand the meaning of Cash discount and effect of cash discount.

- Understand the types of Cash Book.

- Record the transactions in the Cash Book.

3.1   CASH BOOK

This records all receipts of and payments in cash. Usually the deposits into bank accounts maintained by the business, withdrawals from such accounts and cheques payments are also recorded in the Cash Book. Sometimes a separate book for recording receipts and payments by cheques / DDs etc., is kept known as the Bank Book. A Cash Book which is used to record both cash and bank transactions is referred to as a Two-column Cash Book. The format of this cash book is given below:

Illustration 1

Cash Book of Anand & Co.

Dr.   Cr.

Date	Receipts	Ledger Folio	Cash	Bank	Date	Payments	Ledger Folio	Cash	Bank
2008					2008				
July 1	To Balance b/f		11,500	13,000	July 2	By Wages		150	
6			1,800		5	By Electricity			800
7	To Sales			7,000		By Salaries			
11	To Z & Co.			2,000	8	By O Ltd		4,400	11,200
30					15	By Plant		4,000	
	To R.K. Corporation To Sales		2,500		22	By Balance		7,250	10,000
					31	c/f			
			15,800	22,000				15,800	22,00

3.2 CASH DISCOUNTS

Sometimes, in order to encourage early payments due from customers, a company may offer a certain percentage of the amount as a discount. For example, if a customer owes the company Rs. 11,000, the company may allow 3% discount if the payment is made before a certain date. In such a case, the customer would pay an actual cash of Rs. 10,670 only (Rs. 11000-3% of Rs. 11,000) and Rs. 330 would be treated as discount expense by the company. A cash discount may be distinguished from a trade discount which is given on the invoice price, especially when orders for large quantities are placed. The trade discount is therefore reflected as a reduction in the sale price itself. Therefore Trade discount not recorded in books of Accounts.

A cash book can also be used to record the cash discounts that are allowed to customers for prompt payments and the cash discounts that are earned on payments made to suppliers within a stipulated time period. Since discounts will be allowed to customers at the time of receipt of money and received from suppliers at the time of payment of dues, it is convenient to maintain the column for discounts allowed on the receipts side of the cash book and the column for discounts received on the payments side. A cash book in which the cash and bank transactions and the details of cash discounts are recorded is referred to as a Three-column cash book. An illustrative format of this type of cash book is given below:

Illustration 2

Cash Book of Anand & Co.

Dr.   **Cr.**

Date	Receipts	Discount allowed	Cash	Bank	Date	Payments	Discount received	Cash	Bank
201					2010				
Apri					Apri				
1	To Balance		11,500	6,50 0	1	By Salaries			6,200
1	b/f		8,000		1	By Wages		2,50 0	
6	To Sales	100			3	By Printing			4,000
7	To Z & Co.	100	600	10,00 0	5	By Repairs			
11	To Balu				8	By K Ltd	100	4,00 0	10,900
20	Corpn. To		1,500	22,35 0	15	By			4,00 0
	Sales				20	Drawings		12,700	
		200	21,60	38,85			100	21,600	38,85

Illustration: 3

Enter the following transactions in simple cash book. April,

2010

1 Started business with Cash Rs. 50,000

3 Made Cash purchases Rs. 8,000

4 Made Cash Sales Rs. 12,000

6 Purchased furniture Rs. 4,000

7 Received Cash from Mr. Kulkarni Rs. 8,000

8 Paid Salaries Rs. 5,000

Cash Book

Dr.   **Cr.**

Date	Particulars	V. No.	JF No	Rs.	Date	Particulars	V. No.	JF No	Rs.
2010					2010				
April,					April,				
1	To Capital A/c			50,000	3	By Purchases A/c			8,000
4	To Sales A/c			12,000	6	By Furniture A/c			4,000
7	To Kulkarni''s A/c			8,000	8	By Salaries A/c			5,000
					30	By bal. c/d			53,000
				70,000					**70,000**

3.3   PETTY CASH BOOK

When the petty cash fund is operated as an imprest fund, the recording of the petty expenses paid will be made in the petty cash book. This would also avoid recording too many small value transactions in the main cash book. The petty cash book would contain a number of analytical columns for grouping the various expenses under a few classifications which would facilitate subsequent posting into the General Ledger. A specimen petty cash book is given below:

Illustration 1:

Analytical Petty Cash Book of Anand & Co.

Amount	Date	Particulars	Total Amo	Postage	Printing &	Carriage	Traveling	Sundry
	2010							
3000	April, 1	To Bank A/c (Cheque encashed)	190	190	232			
	April, 7		232					
		By Postal stamps	616			616		
	April, 10	By Stationery	400	10	206		400	
	April, 15	By Carriage	10					
	April, 20	By Auto fare of salesman	110					
	April, 22	By Telegrams	206					110
	April, 27							
	April, 30	By Carriage By Stationery	1764	200	438	616	400	110
300	April, 30	By Balance c/d	1236					
1236	2010 May, 1	To Balance b/d						
1764	May, 1	To Bank A/c (Cheque encashed)						

Separate Petty Cash A/c is open in Ledger & total Exp. credited to Petty Cash A/c. Individual expenses total is debited to concerned expenses A/c in the Ledger.

3.4   THREE COLUMN CASH BOOK

Cash book with Discount, cash and bank column is known as three column cash-book. In this cash book along with cash transactions banking transactions are also recorded.

Dr. Receipts   Cash book   Payments   Cr.

Date	Particulars	R No	LF No	Disc	Cash	Bank	Date	Particulars	R No	LF No	Discount	Cash	Bank

Journal Entries for cash and Banking Transactions
Accounting Entry

Amount into the book	To the customer
1) Investment of capital in cash by proprietor	Cash A/c ......Dr. To Capital A/c
2) Sale of goods on cash basis	Cash A/c ......Dr. To sales A/c
3) Receipt of Income in cash	Cash A/c ......Dr. To Income A/c
4) Cash deposited in to the Bank	Bank A/c ......Dr. To Cash A/c
5) Cash withdrawn from Bank for office use	Cash A/c .....Dr. To Bank A/c
6) Sale of goods and amount received by Cheque and same cheque is deposited into Bank immediately.	Bank A/c .....Dr. To Sales A/c
7) When bearer cheque is received from outside party.	Cash A/c ....Dr. To Party"s A/c
8) When order or crossed cheque received from outside party.	Bank A/c ......Dr. To Party"s A/c
9) When cheque received from outside Party and deposited in into the bank on the same day	Bank A/c ......Dr. To Party"s A/c
10) Cheque received on earlier day and deposited to day	Bank A/c .....Dr. To Cash A/c
11) Cheque issued to other Party Dishonoured	Bank A/c .....Dr. To Party"s A/c

12) When customer directly deposits the	Bank A/c .....Dr.
13) When bank collects our income and	Bank A/c ......Dr.
14) Cheque received, deposited and then	Party"s A/c ......Dr.
15) Purchase of goods on cash basis / cash	Purchases A/c ....Dr.
16) Payment of expenses in cash	Expenses A/c ....Dr.
17) Entry for Bank charges and commissions	Bank charges A/c..Dr.
18) Transfer of amount from current A/c to	Fixed Deposit A/c .Dr
19) When cheque is issued to outside Party	Party"s A/c ....Dr.

Illustration 2:

During January 2010 Ram transacted the following business:

2010 Jan		Rs.
1.	Commenced business with cash Purchased	20,000
2.	goods on credit from Nadu. Purchased	1,00,000
3.	goods for cash	4,000
4.	Paid Gopal an advance for goods ordered	10,000
5.	Received cash from Maruti as advance for goods ordered by him	6,000
6.	Purchased furniture, office use for cash	2,000
7.	Paid Rent	1,000
8.	Received commission (in cash)	1,600
9.	Goods returned to Nadu	2,000
10.	Goods sold to Kishore	10,000
11.	Paid for postage and telegrams	200
13.	Goods returned by Kishore	2,000
14.	Purchase furniture (amount cheque paid)	16,000
15.	Paid for stationery	1,200
18.	Paid into Bank	5,000
20.	Goods sold for cash	27,750
22.	Bought goods for cash	3,000
25.	Paid salaries by cheque	3,200
28.	Paid rent	1,000
31.	Drew cash for personal use	4,000
32.	Deposited cash into Bank	12,000

Journal Entries in the books of Ram

Date	Particulars	L.F.	Dr. Rs.	Cr. Rs.
2010				
Jan. 1	Cash A/c ....Dr. To Ram"s Capital A/c (Being the cash brought into business as capital)		20,000	20,000
Jan. 2	Purchase A/c ....Dr. To Nandu"s A/c (Being the goods purchased on credit)		1,00,000	1,00,000
Jan. 3	Purchases A/c .....Dr. To Cash A/c (Being the goods purchased for cash)		4,000	4,000
Jan. 4	Gopal A/c .....Dr. To Cash A/c (Being the amount paid to Gopal)		10,000	10,000
Jan. 5	Cash A/c .....Dr. To Maruti A/c (Being the cash received from Maruti)		6,000	6,000
Jan. 6	Furniture A/c .....Dr. To Cash Λ/c (Being the furniture purchased for office use for cash)		2,000	2,000
Jan. 7	Rent A/c ......Dr. To Cash A/c (Being the wages paid)		1,000	1,000

Jan. 8	Cash A/c ......Dr. To Commission Received A/c (Being the commission received)		1,600	1,600
Jan. 9	Nandu A/c .....Dr. To Purchase return A/c (Being goods returned to Nandu)		2,000	2,000
Jan. 10	Kishore A/c ......Dr. To Sales A/c (Being goods sold to Kamal on credit)		10,000	10,000
Jan. 12	Postages & Telegrams A/c..Dr To Cash A/c (Being the amount paid for postages & Telegrams)		200	200
Jan. 13	Sales returns A/c ...Dr. To Kishore"s A/c (Being the goods returned by Kamal)		2,000	2,000
Jan. 14	Furniture A/c .....Dr. To Bank A/c (Being cheque issued for purchase of Furniture)		16,000	16,000
Jan. 15	Stationery A/c ......Dr. To Cash A/c (Being the amount paid for stationery)		1,200	1,200
Jan. 18	Bank A/c ......Dr. To Cash A/c (Being the amount deposited into the Bank)		5,000	5,000
Jan. 20	Cash A/c ....Dr. To Sales A/c (Being the goods sold for cash)		27,750	27,750
Jan. 22	Purchases A/c .....Dr. To Cash A/c (Being the goods purchased for cash)		3,000	3,000

Date	Particulars	L.F.	Dr.	Cr.
Jan. 25	Salaries A/c .....Dr.		3,200	
	To Bank A/c			3,200
	(Being the amount paid as salaries)			
Jan. 28	Rent A/c ......Dr.		1,000	
	To Cash A/c			1,000
	(Being the rent paid)			
Jan. 31	Ram Drawings A/c ..Dr.		4,000	
	To Cash A/c			4,000
	(Being the cash drawn for personal use)			
Jan. 31	Bank A/c .....Dr.		12,000	
	To Cash A/c			12,000
	(Being cash deposited)			

Posting in the Ledger Accounts:

Now let us prepare the ledger accounts based on the entries passed earlier. A separate account is opened in ledger for each account. All the debit entries and credit entries are duly entered. At the end, the accounts are properly balanced. In other words, the total of all debit entries is adjusted against the total of credit entries and balance is carried forward to the next accounting period.

In the Books of Ram
Cash Book, Subsidiary Books and General Ledger
Cash Book
(Three Column)

Date	Receipts	L.F	Cash Rs	Bank Rs	Date	Payments	L.F	Cash Rs	Bank Rs
201					2010				
Jan. 1	To Capital A/c		20,000		Jan. 3	By Purchases A/c		4,000	
Jan. 5	To Maruti's A/c	C	6,000	5,000	Jan. 4	By Gopal A/c		10,000	
Jan. 8	To Commission A/c		1,600			By Furniture A/c		2,000	
Jan. 18	To Cash A/c	C	-	12,000	Jan. 6	By Rent A/c		1,000	16,000
Jan. 20	To Sales A/c		27,750		Jan. 7	By Postage A/c	C	200	
Jan. 31	To Cash A/c	C	-		Jan. 12	By Furniture A/c		1,200	
					Jan. 14	By Stationery A/c	C	5,000	3,200
					Jan. 15	By Bank A/c		3,000	
					Jan. 18	By Purchases		1,000	12,000
								12,000	
								4,000	
			55,350	17,000				55,350	17,000

Note: The letter „C" in the Ledger Folio column denotes a „contra entry". That is an entry for which the debit and credit aspects are found in the Cash Book itself.

Purchases Book

Date	Name of Supplier	Ledger Folio	Inward Invoice No.	Amount Rs.
2010				
Jan.2	Nandu			1,00,000
			Total	**1,00,000**

Purchase Returns Book

Date	Name of Supplier	Ledger Folio	Debit Note No.	Amount Rs.
2010				
Jan.9	Nandu			2,000
			Total	**2,000**

Sales Book

Date	Name of Customer	Ledger Folio	Outward Invoice No.	Amount Rs.
2010				
Jan.10	Kishore			10,000
			Total	**10,000**

Sales Returns Book

Date	Name of Customer	Ledger Folio	Credit Note No.	Amount Rs.
2010				
Jan.13	Kishore			2,000
			Total	**2,000**

General Ledger

Ram's Capital A/c

Dr.   Cr.

Date	Particulars	JF No	Amount	Date	Particulars	JF No	Amount
2010				2010			
Jan.31	To Balance c/d		20,000	Jan.1	By Cash A/c		20,000
			20,000				**20,000**
				Feb.1	By Balance b/d		20,000

Nandus A/c

Dr.   **Cr.**

Date	Particulars	JF No	Amount	Date	Particulars	JF No	Amount
2010				2010			
Jan.9	To Purchase Returns A/c		2,000	Jan.2	By Purchases A/c		1,00,000
Jan.31	To Balance c/d		98,000				
			1,00,000				**1,00,000**
				Feb.1	By Balance b/d		98,000

Purchases A/c

Dr.   **Cr.**

Date	Particulars	JF No	Amount Rs.	Date	Particulars	JF No	Amount Rs.
2010				2010			
Jan.2	To Nandu"s A/c		1,00,000	Jan.31	By Balance c/d		1,07,000
Jan.3	To Cash A/c		4,000				
Jan.22	To Cash A/c		3,000				
			1,07,000				**1,07,000**
Feb.1	To Balance b/d		1,07,000				

Sales A/c

Dr.   **Cr.**

Date	Particulars	JF No	Amount Rs.	Date	Particulars	JF No	Amount Rs.
2010				2010			
Jan.31	To Balance c/d		37,750	Jan.13	By Kishore"s A/c		10,000
				Jan.20	By Cash A/c		27,750
			37,750				**37,750**
				Feb.1	By Balance b/d		37,750

Purchase Return A/c

Dr.   **Cr.**

Date	Particulars	JF No	Amount	Date	Particulars	JF No	Amount
2010				2010			
Jan.31	To Balance c/d		2,000	Jan.9	By Nandu"s A/c		2,000
			2,000				**2,000**
				Feb.1	By Balance b/d		2,000

Sales Return A/c

Dr.							Cr.
Date	Particulars	JF No	Amount Rs.	Date	Particulars	JF No	Amount Rs.
2010				2010			
Jan.13	To Kishore"s A/c		2,000	Jan.31	By Balance c/d		2,000
			2,000				**2,000**
Feb.1	To Balance b/d		2,000				

Gopal's A/c

Dr.   **Cr.**

Date	Particulars	JF No	Amount Rs.	Date	Particulars	JF No	Amount Rs.
2010				2010			
Jan.6	To Cash A/c		10,000	Jan.31	By Balance c/d		10,000
			10,000				**10,000**
Feb.1	To Balance b/d		10,000				

Rent A/c

Date	Particulars	JF No	Amount Rs.	Date	Particulars	JF No	Amount Rs.
2010				2010			
Jan.7	To Cash A/c		1,000	Jan.31	By Balance c/d		1,000
			1,000				**1,000**
Feb.1	To Balance b/d		1,000				

Commission Received A/c

Date	Particulars	JF No	Amount Rs.	Date	Particulars	JF No	Amount Rs.
2010				2010			
Jan.1	To Balance c/d		1,600	Jan.31	By Cash c/d		1,600
			1,600				**1,600**
				Feb.1	By Balance b/d		1,600

Kishore's A/c

Dr.   **Cr.**

Date	Particulars	JF No	Amount Rs.	Date	Particulars	JF No	Amount Rs.
2010				2010			
Jan.10	To Sales A/c		10,000	Jan.31	By Sales Returns A/c		2,000
				Jan.31	By Balance c/d		8,000
			10,000				**10,000**
Feb.1	To Balance b/d		8,000				

Postage & Telegram A/c

Dr.   **Cr.**

Date	Particulars	JF No	Amount Rs.	Date	Particulars	JF No	Amount Rs.
2010				2010			
Jan.12	To Cash A/c		200	Jan.31	By Balance c/d		200
			200				**200**
Feb.1	To Balance b/d		200				

Stationery A/c Salaries A/c

Dr.   **Cr.**

Date	Particulars	JF No	Amount Rs.	Date	Particulars	JF No	Amount Rs.
2010				2010			
Jan.15	To Cash A/c		1,200	Jan.31	By Balance c/d		1,200
			1,200				**1,200**
Feb.1	To Balance b/d		1,200				

Dr.   **Cr.**

Date	Particulars	JF No	Amount Rs.	Date	Particulars	JF No	Amount Rs.
2010				2010			
Jan.25	To Bank A/c		3,200	Jan.31	By Balance c/d		3,200
			3,200				**3,200**
Feb.1	To Balance b/d		3,200				

Rent A/c

Date	Particulars	JF No	Amount Rs.	Date	Particulars	JF No	Amount Rs.
2010				2010			
Jan.28	To Cash A/c		1,000	Jan.31	By Balance c/d		1,000
			1,000				**1,000**
Feb. 1	To Balance b/d		1,000				

Drawings A/c

Date	Particulars	JF No	Amount Rs.	Date	Particulars	JF No	Amount Rs.
2010				2010			
Jan.31	To Cash A/c		4,000	Jan.31	By Balance c/d		4,000
			4,000				**4,000**
Feb.1	To Balance b/d		4,000				

Maruti's A/c

Date	Particulars	JF No	Amount Rs.	Date	Particulars	JF No	Amount Rs.
2010				2010			
Jan.31	To Balance c/d		6,000	Jan.5	By Cash A/c		6,000
			6,000				**6,000**
				Feb.1	By Balance b/d		6,000

Furniture A/c

Date	Particulars	JF No	Amount Rs.	Date	Particulars	JF No	Amount Rs.
2010				2010			
Jan.6	To Cash A/c		2,000	Jan.31	By Balance c/d		2,000
			2,000				**2,000**
Feb. 1	To Balance b/d		2,000				

3.5. EXERCISES

3.5.1 Theory Questions

7. Explain term „Book Keeping.
8. What is Account?
9. Distinguish between:
   a) Book-keeping and Accountancy
   b) Personal Accounts and impersonal Accounts c) Real Accounts and Nominal Accounts
   d) Single Entry system and Double Entry system
   e) Cash system of Accounts and Accrual system of Accounts.
10. Discuss the principles of debit and credit of Accounts.
11. Explain Journal & its utility.
12. What is Ledger? What is a ledger Account?
13. Explain how a ledger account is balance? What is indicates by Debit or Credit balance?
14. "By sub-division of journal, there will be a division of labour". Explain.
15. Which type of transactions will be recorded in sales Book and purchase Book.
16. What is cash Book? What are different types of cash book.
17. What do you mean by "Contra Entries" in the cash book with Cash & Bank columns?
18. What is the petty cash?

1) Journalise the following transactions in the books of Ram for the month of March 2010.

March 1 Ram commenced business with cash Rs. 60,000.

2 Purchased furniture for Rs. 5,000.

4 Purchased goods for cash Rs. 2,000.

7 Bought goods from M/s. Raj & Co. for Rs. 4,000.

10 Sold goods costing Rs. 3,000 on cash.

15 Purchased stationery for office use Rs. 1,000.

19 Received cash Rs. 1,250 from Mr. Ketan in full settlement of his account for Rs. 1,500.

20 Paid salaries by cheque Rs. 1,500.

25 Introduced additional capital Rs. 20,000.

27 Paid to Raj Rs. 3,250 in full settlement of Rs. 3,500

29 Sold goods for Rs. 15,000 to Mr. Dohi.

31 Deposited Rs. 3,000 into the Bank.

2) Journalise the following transactions in the books of Mr. Shiva for the month of April 2010.

April 1 Started business with cash Rs. 25,000/-

6 Purchased goods worth Rs. 10,000/-

4 Deposited cash Rs. 3,000 into the Bank.

6 Purchased goods of Rs. 6,000 from M/s. Raju Trading Company.

9 Sold goods to Mr. Ramesh for Rs. 3,000.

12 Paid to M/s. Raju Trading Company Rs. 3,000.

15 Received Rs. 1,000 from Mr. Ramesh.

20 Paid salaries Rs. 1,000/- and paid commission Rs. 1,600/- in cash.

25 Bought stationery for office use Rs. 300.

27 Withdrew Rs. 2,500 from business for personal use.

29 Withdrew Rs. 4,000 from bank for office use.

3) Journalise the following transactions in the journal of Mr. Anand for the month of February, 2010.

Feb 1 Borrowed from Bank @ 15% interest Rs. 20,000.

7 Purchased goods from Mr. Sam for Rs. 3,500.

8 Paid carriage and cartage Rs. 250

9 Sold goods on cash Rs. 3,000.

11 Paid Rs. 2,250 to Mr. Sam.

16 Purchased office furniture for Rs. 6,000.

19 Paid interest Rs. 450/- to Mr. Bank.

20 Paid salaries Rs. 6,000.

22 Cash sales Rs. 20,000.

26 Cash purchases Rs. 15,000

28 Paid Rs. 2,000 to Bank in part payment of loan.

Unit - 4

BANK RECONCILIATION STATEMENT

Unit Structure:

4.0   OBJECTIVES

After studying the unit the students will be able to:

- Define and explain bank reconciliation statement.
- Know the reasons of disagreement of the balances of cash book and bank statement.
- Prepare the format of the statement.
- Prepare bank reconciliation statement.

4.1   MEANING

A customer of the bank opens a Bank Account in his Cash book to record all his bank transactions. Similarly a bank maintains a Customer"s Account in its ledger, and gives a Bank Pass Book to the customer. From the entries in the pass book a customer can have knowledge of the transactions recorded by the bank in his account. When we make entries on the debit side of Bank Account the bank makes entries on the credit side of our account for the same transactions and vice versa. As a result when the Bank Account shows debit balance, the pass book shows credit balance and vice-versa.

As a matter of fact balance shown by the Bank Account and by the bank pass book on a particular day must tally. But in actual practice they differ due to reasons given below. It is therefore, becomes necessary to reconcile the difference to ascertain that there are no mistakes committed. Thus a Bank Reconciliation Statement is a statement prepared to reconcile the difference between the balances as shown by the Bank Account in a Cash Book and by the Bank Pass Book.

4.2 REASONS FOR DIFFERENCES IN BANK BALANCE OF CASH BOOK WITH PASS BOOK

Some of the transactions are entered in the Cash Book (Bank column only) whereas some are entered only in the Pass Book. In addition to this there may be some mistakes committed, either in the Cash book or in the Pass Book.

A) Transactions entered in the Cash Book (Bank Column) or in the pass book.

   i) Cheques issued: When a cheque is issued, Bank Account is at once credited, but the Customers Account is debited by the Banker only when the payment of that cheque is effected by the Bank.

   ii) Cheques paid or deposited into the Bank : When a cheque is received and paid into the bank, the customer debits at once the Bank Account in his Cash Book, but the Customer"s Account is credited by the Banker only when the cheque is collected by the bank.

B) Generally the following transactions are entered first in the Pass Book and subsequently they are entered in the Cash Book from the Pass Book.

1. Bank Charges

2. Interest allowed or charged by Bank

3. Dividend, Interest on Investment collected by Bank on behalf of a customer.

4. Dishonour of cheque paid into Bank and credited to Customer"s Account by Bank.

5. Amount collected or paid for Bills of Exchange by Bank, Sale of Securities on behalf of a customer.

6. Payment by Bank, such as Club Subscription, Insurance Premium, Purchases of Securities on behalf of a customer.

4.3 PREPARATION OF BANK RECONCILIATION STATEMENT

In actual practice, we have both Cash Book (Bank Account) and the Bank Pass Book on hand, to compare the entries in them during a particular period. As the entries which are made in both the books do not cause the difference in balance, they are to be left out. The entries which are recorded only in one of the two books are taken into consideration.

Generally, Bank balance either as per Cash Book or as per Pass Book of a particular date is given and the balance as per other book is required to be traced out.

A) First ascertain balance that is whether a debit balance or a credit balance.

B) Out of the transactions given, those which are recorded in both the books that is Cash Book and Pass Book before the date of reconciliation are not to be considered.

C) Transaction which is recorded in only one of two books either in the Cash Book or in the Pass Book is to be considered.

Bank Reconciliation Statements helps the customer to know which cheques are yet to be realized and which cheques are not yet encashed.

It reduces the chances of misappropriation by the Bank employees.

4.4 CHART FOR SOLVING THE PROBLEMS

The following charts will help the students in solving the problems:

Transactions	Given Bank balance as per Cash Book or overdraft as per Pass Book	Given Bank balance as per Pass Book or overdraft as per Cash Book
1. Cheques issued but not encashed recorded in the Cash Book only.	Add	Less
2. Interest allowed or collected by Bank, Sale of Investments recorded in Pass Book only.	Add	Less
3. Direct payment into bank by our customer etc.	Add	Less

4. Wrong amount taken in Cash Book		
i) Short Amount	Add	Less
ii) Excess Amount	Less	Add
5. Cheque paid into Bank but not credited by Bank.	Less	Add
6. Bank Charges, Interest charged by Bank or dishonour of cheque etc. are recorded in Pass Book only.	Less	Add
7. Bank charges, Interest charged by Bank or dishonour of cheqe etc. are recorded in Pass Book only.	Less	Add
8. Payment by bank for insurance premium, club subscription, Purchase of Securities etc. are recorded in Pass Book only.	Less	Add

4.5 SPECIMEN OF BANK RECONCILIATION STATEMENT

Particulars	Rs.	Rs.
Balance as per Cash / Pass Book given		XX
Add : The transaction that would increase the balance in the other Book.	XX	XX
Less : The transaction that would reduce the balance of the other book	XX	(XX)
Balance as per Cash / Pass Book (i.e. other book) as on		XXX

4.6 BANK OVERDRAFT

Normally, Traders keeps depositing cash into Bank Account and withdraws by issuing cheques to various parties. However, trader makes arrangement with the bank, to withdraw more than his bank balance. This is known as Bank Overdraft. The upper limit of such overdraft is fixed in advance. When there is overdraft Bank Account in trader"s books shows credit balance and in the books of Bank, trader"s account will show debit balance, and he is a debtor.

For preparing reconciliation statement, taking Bank overdraft as base, it will be exact opposite that of Bank Balance, add items will become Less and less items will be Add.

4.7 IMPORTANCE OF BANK RECONCILIATION STATEMENT

After getting Bank Statement / Pass Book, businessmen, compares entries in Cash Book (recorded by trader) and Bank Statement (recorded by bank in relation to businessmen) and prepare Bank Reconciliation. While preparing reconciliation statement, numbers of entries are not matching with each other these discrepancies may lead to notice frauds, errors, misappropriation of cash, by cashier. It reduces the charges of misappropriation by the employees, so timely action may be taken. At the same time, it is possible that Bank might have made wrong entry of deposit or withdrawal, businessmen can be inform bank to correct it.

It presents sinero, of e-banking of increasing use of credit card / debit card facilities / Net banking. Their may be number of transaction are not recorded in time which can be brought to notice. For wrong entry by bank, immediate action can be taken, asking bank to verify the mistake(s).

CHECK YOUR PROGRESS

- Give the examples of various transactions which are generally entered first in the Pass Book.

- If the Bank balance as per Cash Book is given, how the following transactions affect:

    1. Interest allowed or collected by Bank, Sale of Investments recorded in Pass Book only.

    2. Cheque paid into Bank but not credited by Bank.

    3. Payments by bank for insurance premium, club subscription, Purchase of Securities etc. are recorded in Pass Book only.

    4. Direct payment into bank by our customer.

    5. Bank Charges, Interest charged by Bank or dishonour of cheque etc. are recorded in Pass Book only.

4.8 ILLUSTRATIONS

Illustration 1 : On 31st December 2010, M/s. M.D. & Co."s bank column of Cash Book showed a debit balance Rs.17,800/- from the following particulars prepare a Bank Reconciliation Statement showing the balance as per Bank Pass Book as on 31st December 2010.

1. Cheques deposited into the Bank but not cleared and credited before 31st December amounted to Rs.8,950/-.

2. Cheques issued on 31st December but presented for payment on the 7th January 2011 amounted to Rs.6,750/-.

3. Purchases of securities of Rs.4,000/- by the Bank on behalf of M/s. M.D. & Co. appeared in Pass Book only.

4. Interest Rs.95/- was credited in the Pass Book but was entered in the Cash Book as Rs.59/-.

5. Bank charges Rs.45/- were recorded in the Pass Book but no entry was made in the Cash Book.

Bank Reconciliation Statement as on 31-12-2010

Particulars	Rs.	Rs.
Balance at the bank as per Cash Book as on 31-12-2010.		17,800
Add :		
(i) Cheques issued on 31st December but not cashed upto 31st December 2010.	6,750	
(ii) Interest recorded in the Cash Book as Rs.59/- instead of Rs.95/-, hence the difference.	36	6,786
		24,586
Less :		
(i) Cheques paid into Bank but not cleared upto 31st December 2010.	8,950	
(ii) Payment made by Bank for purchase of securities not entered in the Cash Book.	4,000	
(iii) Bank charges appearing in the Pass Book.	45	(6,390)
Balance as per Pass Book as on 31st December 2010.		8,710

Illustration 2 : On 30th June, 2010 the Cash Book of M/s. Patil & Co. showed a Bank balance of Rs.12,000/-.

1. Cheques sent to Bank for collection of Rs.10,000/- before 30-06-2010 but only one cheque of Rs.4,000/- is credited in June 2010.

2. Cheque issued for Rs.5,000/- in the month of June, but cheques of Rs.2,500/- presented for payment in July 2010.

3. The following entries were passed in the Pass Book before 30th June, 2010 but no corresponding entry was made in the Cash Book.

   a) Rs.320/- paid a Insurance Premium.

   b) Interest on Investment collected by the Bank Rs.600/-.

   c) Bank has charged Rs.50/- as interest and commission Rs.20/-.

Prepare a Bank Reconciliation Statement as on 30th June, 2010 from the above particulars.

Solution :

Bank Reconciliation Statement as on 30-06-2010

Particulars	Rs.	Rs.
Balance as per Cash Book as on 30-06-2010.		12,000
Add :		
(i) Cheques issued but not encashed before 30th June 2010.	2,500	
(ii) Interest collected by Bank.	600	3,100
		15,100
Less :		
(i) Cheques paid in to Bank but not credited by Bank.	6,000	
(ii) Insurance Premium paid by Bank.	320	
(iii) Interest and Commission charged by Bank.	70	(6,390)
Balance as per Pass Book as on 3-06-2010.		8,710

4.9   EXERCISES

4.9.1 Theory Questions :

i) What is Bank Reconciliation Statement?

ii) What are different reasons for disagreement between Bank balance as per Cash Book & Pass Book / Bank Statement?

iii) Discuss procedure for preparation of Bank Reconciliation Statement.

iv) A Trader feels that it is not necessary to prepare Bank Reconciliation Statement, do you as Finance Manager agrees with trader? Why?

v) Discuss need of preparing Bank Reconciliation Statement.

4.9.2 Practical problems:

1) The Cash Book of Mr. Raj shows a balance of Rs.26,700/- on 31st October, 2011. From the following information you are required to prepare a Bank Reconciliation Statement as on 31st October, 2010.

    i) A cheque of Rs.5,000/- received from Miss Varma, deposited into the Bank but not yet credited in the Pass Book by the bank.

    ii) A cheque of Rs.6,000/- drawn in favour of Miss Meena, had not been presented into the Bank.

    iii) As per our instruction the bank had a promissory note of Rs.1,000/-. It is not yet recorded in the Cash Book.

    iv) A cheque of Rs.7,500/- received from Mr. Madhu recorded in the Cash Book, but the same cheque was sent to the bank on 1st November, 2010.

    v) Bank collected proceeds of Bill Receivable amounted to Rs.5,500/- and credited in the Pass Book but not yet recorded in the Cash Book.

    vi) Post dated cheque amounted to Rs.10,500/- issued to Mr. Shanti, recorded in the Cash Book but not yet presented to the bank.

    vii) Pass Book shows credit entries in respect of Rs.4,500/- as interest collected on investment and Rs.2,000/- as dividend collected by bank. These were not recorded in the Cash Book.

2) Prepare Bank Reconciliation Statement as on 31st January, 2011 from the following particulars.

    i) Bank balance as per Cash Book Rs.22,510/-.

    ii) Cheque amounted to Rs.13,500/- sent to the bank for collection as on 28th January, 2010 but collected by the bank as on 2nd February, 2010.

    iii) Bank column of Cash Book credit side cast short by Rs.2,250/-.

    iv) Cheques of Rs.7,500/- deposited into the bank and collected by the bank and credited in the Pass Book but recorded twice in the Cash Book.

    v) Cheques of Rs.16,000/- issued in favour of Mr. Rane returned dishonoured for lack of fund. Dishonour of cheque not yet recorded in the Cash Book.

vi) Proprietor has closed his savings account and transferred the balance of Rs.9,500/- to current account, not recorded in Cash Book.

vii) Bank Pass Book shows debit entry for payment of electricity charges of Rs.1,800/- and credit entry of Rs.9,500/- for collection of salaries. Corresponding entries were not found in the Cash Book.

3) On 31st December, 2010 the Cash Book showed an overdraft of Rs.16,600/-. From the following particulars, prepare Bank Reconciliation Statement as on 31st December, 2010.

i) Cheques paid into the bank but not cleared Rs.4,040/-. ii)

Cheques drawn but not cashed for Rs.3,100/-.

iii) A Bill Receivable for Rs.1,500/- previously discounted with the bank had been dishonoured and debited in the Pass Book along with bank charges Rs.100/-.

iv) Pass Book debit total undercasted by Rs.100/- whereas credit total of Cash Book under.

v) Interest on Bank overdraft amounting Rs.6,750/- not accounted in Cash Book.

vi) ECS claring for telephone charges Rs.710 not accounted in Cash Book.

vii) Debit total of Cash Book Page No. 11 = Rs.3,100/- wrongly carried on credit side of Cash Book.

Unit - 5

LEDGER AND TRIAL BALANCE

Unit Structure:

5.0   OBJECTIVES

After studying the unit the students will be able to:

- Know the meaning of Ledger.

- Understand the process of opening a Ledger Account.

- Prepare a Ledger Account from the given information.

- Explain the types of Trial Balance.

- Prepare the Trial Balance from the balances given.

5.1   MEANING

The ledger is the principal book of accounts relating to a particular person or property or revenue or expenses are recorded in summarized form. It is a set of accounts. It contains all accounts of the business enterprise whether real, nominal or personal. The main function of a ledger is to classify or sort out all items appearing in the journal or other subsidiary books under their appropriate accounts & that at the end of the accounting period each account will contain the entire information of all the transactions relating to in a summarized or condensed form.

All the transactions are recorded first in the journal and then from the journal they are posted in the respective accounts in the ledger. Ledger is a book where in all the transactions would ultimately find their place under the respective heads of accounts. Ledger is a book of final entry.

5.2   HOW TO OPEN AN ACCOUNT IN THE LEDGER :

The pages of all books of accounts must be numbered to facilitate reference. The page is divided into two parts by vertical line in between. The left hand side is used as a debit side of an account and the right hand side is used as a credit side.

_____Name (Account)

Dr.   Cr.

Date	Particulars	J.F.	Amt.	Date	Particulars	J.F.	Amt.

5.3   POSTING :

Every transaction is first recorded in the book of original entry and then it is posted into the ledger. Posting is made to the debit side account which is debited in the journal entry and to the credit side of an account which is credited in the journal entry. Name of the credit account is written on the debit account and the name of debit account is written on the credit side of account. Entry on the debit side of an account starts with "To" whereas on the credit side starts with "By".

5.4   BALANCE AND BALANCING OF ACCOUNTS :

The object of recording the business transactions in various ledger accounts to enable a trader to ascertain balance in account easily at any time. For the preparation of Trial balance all accounts are to be closed.

Each account in the ledger may have same entries on the debit side and some entries on the credit side of an account. Find out difference between totals of each side.

The difference in the total of both the side is termed as Balance of an account. The process of extracting the balance and inserting it on lesser side of an account is called balancing or closing of an account.

Types of Balances

A) Debit Balance : If the debit side of an account is heavier than its credit side, the balance is called debit balance.

B) Credit Balance : If the credit side of an account is heavier than its debit side, the balance is called credit balance.

5.5 MEANING OF BALANCES :

5.5.1 Personal Accounts : Personal Accounts may have debit or credit balance.

Debit balance shows that person owes to the firm. He is debtors. Credit balance shows that persons owed to him. He is creditor.

5.5.2 Real Accounts : Real accounts always have debit balance. These are value of Assets, properties owned by businessmen.

5.5.3 Nominal Accounts : Nominal Account may have debit or credit balance debit balances shows total expenses / losses for the period. Credit balances shows total income / gain for the period.

At the end of accounting period balances of nominal accounts transferred to Trading, Profit & Loss Account, whereas balances shown of Personal Accounts & Real accounts in the Balance Sheet, and next year these balances considered as opening balances.

CHECK YOUR PROGRESS

- Fill in the blanks:
    1. If the debit side of an account is heavier than its credit side, the balance is called---------------------------.
    2. The left hand side of a Ledger Account is used as a -------------- and the right hand side is used as a --------------------.
    3. -----------------and ---------------- Accounts may have debit or credit balance.
    4. Debit balance of the -----------Account shows that person owes to the firm. It means he is the ------------of the firm.
    5. Credit balances of the Nominal Account shows total --------- -----------------for the period.
    6. Real accounts always have -------------- balance.

- Define Ledger and draw the proforma of Ledger Account.

5.6 ILLUSTRATIONS-1 :

Illustration 1: Enter the following transactions in the proper subsidiary books and post them to the Ledger Accounts and balance the Account 30 June 2010.

1   Commenced business with Cash Rs.5,000/- (of which Rs.2,000/- borrowed from friend Ram) and furniture Rs.1,400/-

2   Purchased goods from Kanta Rs.1,800/- less 5%. Trade Discount.

6   Sold goods to Ketual costing Rs.400/- at 10% Profit.

7   Cash purchases Rs.500/-.

8   Cash sales – Rs.1,200/-.

9   Purchased goods from Baba Rs.500/-.

9   Paid into Bank Rs.2,000/-.

10 Returned to Kanta goods worth Rs.150/-.

11 Purchased office furniture for Rs.1,200/- and paid for same by cheque.

16 Issued a cheque to Kanta for Rs.910/-.

21 Invoiced goods to Ketual Rs.5,000/- less 2% Trade discount.

23 Ketual paid cash Rs.400/- and returned goods of Rs.140/-.

24 Purchased goods from Kanta Rs.1,300/-.

28 Returned damaged goods to Janta Rs.160/- & to Baba Rs.150/-.

28 Sold goods to Kant Rs.1,200/-.

29 Received a cheque for Rs.1,100/- from Kant and banked the same.

30 Kant, who owes us Rs.100/- pays rent Rs.100/- to our landlord on our behalf.

30 We paid Rs.75/- to Raju on instructions from our creditor Kanta on his behalf.

Solution :

Journal

Date	Particulars	L.F.	Debit Rs.	Credit Rs.
2010 June 1	Furniture A/c ……………... …… Dr. To Capital A/c (Furniture brought in by Proprietor.)		1,400	1,400
30	Rent A/c …………………………… Dr. To Kant A/c		100	100

Purchase book

Date	Name of Supplier	Inward Invoiced No.	L.F.	Amount Rs.
2010 June 2	Kanta	-	-	1,710
9	Baba	-	-	500
24	Kanta	-	-	1,300
		Total		3,510

Returns Outward Book

Date	Particulars	Debit Note No.	L.F.	Amount Rs.
2010				
June 10	Kanta	-	-	150
28	Kanta	-	-	160
28	Baba	-	-	150
		Total		**460**

Sales Book

Date	Particulars	Debit Note No.	L.F.	Amount Rs.
2010				
June 6	Ketual	-	-	440
21	Ketual	-	-	4,900
28	Kant	-	-	1,200
		Total		**6,540**

Returns Inward Book

Date	Particulars	Credit Note No.	J.F.	Amount Rs.
2010				
June 23	Ketual	-	-	140
		Total		**140**

Cash Account

Dr.   Cr.

Date	Particulars	L.F.	Bank	Cash	Date	Particulars	L.F.	Bank	Cash
2010					2010				
June 1	To Capital A/c			3,000	June 7	By Purchases A/c			
1	To Ram Loan A/c			2,000	9		C		500
8					11	By Bank A/c			2,000
9	To Sales A/c			1,200	16	By Furniture A/c		1,200	
23	To Cash A/c	C	2,000		30			910	
29	To Ketual A/c To Kant"s A/c		1,100	400	30	By Kanta A/c			75
					30	By Kanta A/c		990	4,025
			3,100	**6,600**		By Balance c/d		**3,100**	**6,600**
July 1			990	4,025					

Capital
Account

Date	Particulars	J.F.	Rs.	Date	Particulars	J.F.	Rs.
2010 June 30	To Balance c/d		4,400	2010 June 1	By Cash A/c By Furniture A/c		3,000 1,400
			4,400				4,400
				July 1	By Balance b/d		4,400

Furniture
Account

Date	Particulars	J.F	Rs.	Date	Particulars	J.F	Rs.
2010 June 30 11	To Capital A/c To Bank A/c		1,400 1,200	2010 June 30	By Balance c/d		2,600
			2,600				2,600
July 1	To Balance b/d		2,600				

Purchases
Account

Date	Particulars	J.F	Rs.	Date	Particulars	J.F	Rs.
2010 June 7 30	To Cash A/c To Sundries A/c (as per purchase Book)		500 3,510	2010 June 30	By Balance c/d		4,010
			4,010				4,010
July 1	To Balance b/d		4,010				

Sales Account

Date	Particulars	J.F	Rs.	Date	Particulars	J.F	Rs.
2010 June 30	To Balance c/d		7,740	2010 June 8 30	By Cash A/c By Sundries A/c		1,200 6,540
			7,740				7,740
				July 1	By Balance b/d		7,740

Return Outward Account

Dr.   Cr.

Date	Particulars	J.F	Rs.	Date	Particulars	J.F	Rs.
2010 June 30	To Balance c/d		460	2010 June 30	By Sundries A/c (as per R. O. Book)		460
			460				460
				July 1	By Balance b/d		460

Return Inward Account

Dr.   Cr.

Date	Particulars	J.F	Rs.	Date	Particulars	J.F	Rs.
2010 June 30	To Balance c/d		140	2010 June 1	By Balance c/d		140
			140				140
July 1	To Balance b/d		140				

Ram's Loan Account

Dr.   Cr.

Date	Particulars	J.F	Rs.	Date	Particulars	J.F	Rs.
2010 June 10	To Balance c/d		2,000	2010 June 1	By Cash A/c		2,000
			2,000				2,000
				July 1	By Balance b/d		2,000

Kanta's Account

Dr.   Cr.

Date	Particulars	J.F	Rs.	Date	Particulars	J.F	Rs.
2010 June 10	To Return Outward A/c		150	2010 June 2	By Purchases A/c		1,710
19	To Bank A/c		910	24	By Purchases A/c		1,300
28	To Returns Outward A/c		160				
30	To Cash A/c		75				
30	To Balance c/d		1,715				
			3,010				3,010
				July 1	By Balance b/d		1,715

64

Ketual's Account

Dr.							Cr.
Date	Particulars	J.F	Rs.	Date	Particulars	J.F	Rs.
2010				2010			
June 6	To Sales A/c		440	June 23	By Return Inward A/c		140
21	To Sales A/c		4,900		By Cash A/c		400
					By Bal. c/d		4,800
			5,340				5,340
July 1	To Balance b/d		4,800				

Rent Account

Dr.							Cr.
Date	Particulars	J.F	Rs.	Date	Particulars	J.F	Rs.
2010				2010			
June 30	To Kant A/c		100	June 30	By Balance c/d		100
			100				100

Baba's Account

Dr.							Cr.
Date	Particulars	J.F	Rs.	Date	Particulars	J.F	Rs.
2010				2010			
June 28	To Return Outward A/c		150	June 9	By Purchases A/c		500
30	To Balance c/d		350	30			
			500				500
				July 1	By Balance b/d		350

Kant's Account

Dr.							Cr.
Date	Particulars	J.F	Rs.	Date	Particulars	J.F	Rs.
2010				2010			
June 28	To Sales A/c		1,200	June 29	By Bank A/c		1,100
					By Rent A/c		100
			1,200				1,200

Illustration 2 :

M. D. as on 1st March 2010

Debit Balance	Rs.	Credit Balance	Rs.
Cash A/c	15,000	Capital A/c	60,000
Bank A/c	12,000	Mr. Chandra A/c	9,000
Stock A/c	14,000		
ZaCo A/c	28,000		

2010

March 2 Borrowed Rs.30,000/- from sister Maya for business purpose.

4 Bought goods from Mr. Chandra for Rs.6,000/- @ 5% trade discount.

7 Sold goods worth Rs.15,000/- to Mr. ZaCo @ 2% trade discount.

9 Received Rs.7,000/- from Mr. ZaCo.

10 Cash deposited into Bank Rs.7,000/-.

12 Paid Rs.5,000/- to Mr. Chandra by issuing a cheque.

15 Paid for new equipment of office Rs.4,000/-.

17 Purchased new furniture for Rs.2,500/- for personal use.

19 Cash purchases Rs.15,000/- and cash sales Rs.27,100/-.

22 Paid salaries Rs.1,700/-, rent Rs,1,250/-, commission Rs.800/- by cash.

26 Withdrew Rs.8,500/- from the business for daughter"s marriage by a cheque.

27 Goods worth Rs.1,000/- withdrawn from the business for house use, out of opening stock.

31 Paid interest Rs.300/- to sister Maya on borrowings.

You are required to journalise the above transactions including Cash / Bank and post them to the ledger and balance the same.

In the books of M.D.

Solution :

Date	Particulars	L. F.	Debit Rs.	Credit Rs.
2010 March 2	Cash A/c .... Dr. To Maya"s Loan A/c		30,000	30,000
4	Purchase A/c .... Dr. To Chandra"s A/c		5,700	5,700
7	ZaCo A/c .... Dr. To Sales A/c (Being cash received from ZaCo.)		14,700	14,700
9	Cash A/c .... Dr. To ZaCo A/c (Being cash received from ZaCo.)		7,000	7,000
10	Bank A/c .... Dr. To Cash A/c (Being cash deposited into Bank.)		7,000	7,000
12	Chandra"s A/c .... Dr. To Bank A/c (Being cheque issued.)		5,000	5,000
15	Office Equipment A/c .... Dr. To Cash A/c (Being office equipment purchased.)		4,000	4,000
17	Drawing A/c ....Dr. To Cash A/c (Being furniture purchased for personal use.)		2,500	2,500
19	Purchases A/c ....Dr. To Cash A/c		15,000	15,000
19	Cash A/c .... Dr. To Sales A/c (Being goods sold.)		27,100	27,100
22	Salaries A/c ....Dr. Rent A/c .... Dr. Commission A/c ....Dr. To Cash A/c (Being Salaries, Rent & Commission paid.)		1,700 1,250 800	3,750

26	Drawing A/c .... Dr.		8,500		
	To Bank A/c			8,500	
	(Being amount withdrawn by cheque				
27	Drawing A/c ....Dr.		1,000		
	To Stock A/c			1,000	
31	Interest A/c .... Dr.		300		
	To Cash A/c			300	

Ledger Accounts
Cash Account

Dr.　　　　　　　　　　　　　　　　　　　　　　　　　　　Cr.

Date	Particulars	J.F	Rs.	Date	Particulars	J.F	Rs.
2010				2010			
Mar 1	To Bal b/d		15,000	Mar 10	By Cash A/c		7,000
2	To Maya"s		30,000	15	By Office		
	Loan A/c			17	Equipment		4,000
	To ZaCo		7,000	19	A/c By Drawings		2,500
19	A/c To		27,100	22	A/c By		15,000
	Sales A/c			22	Purchases A/c		1,700
				22	By Salaries A/c		1,250
				31	By Rent A/c		800
				31	By Commission A/c		300
					By Interest A/c		46,550
			79,100		By Balance c/d		79,100
Apr 1			46,550				

Bank Account

Dr.　　　　　　　　　　　　　　　　　　　　　　　　　　　Cr.

Date	Particulars	J.F	Rs.	Date	Particulars	J.F	Rs.
2010				2010			
Mar 1	To Bal b/d		12,000	Mar 12	By Chandan"s		5,000
10	To Cash A/c		7,000	26	A/c By Drawings		8,500
				37	A/c By Balance c/d		5,500
			19,000				19,000
Apr 1	To Balance b/d		5,500				

Stock Account

Dr.   **Cr.**

Date	Particulars	J.F	Rs.	Date	Particulars	J.F	Rs.
2010 Mar 1	To Bal b/d		14,000	2010 Mar 27	By Drawings A/c		1,000
				31	By Balance c/d		13,000
			14,000				14,000
Apr 1	To Balance b/d		13,000				

Purchase Account

Dr.   **Cr.**

Date	Particulars	J.F	Rs.	Date	Particulars	J.F	Rs.
2010 Mar 1	To Chandra''s A/c		5,700	2010 Mar 31	By Bal c/d		20,700
19	To Cash A/c		15,000				
			20,700				20,700
Apr 1	To Bal b/d		20,700				

Sales Account

Dr.   **Cr.**

Date	Particulars	J.F	Rs.	Date	Particulars	J.F	Rs.
2010 Mar 31	To bal c/d		41,800	2010 Mar 1	By ZaCo A/c		14,700
				31	By Cash A/c		27,100
			41,800				41,800
				Apr 1	By Balance b/d		41,800

Salaries Account

Dr.   **Cr.**

Date	Particulars	J.F	Rs.	Date	Particulars	J.F	Rs.
2010 Mar 22	To Cash A/c		1,700	2010 Mar 31	By Balance c/d		1,700
			1,700				1,700
Apr 1	To Balance b/d		1,700				

Rent Account

Dr.							Cr.
Date	Particulars	J.F	Rs.	Date	Particulars	J.F	Rs.
2010 Mar 22	To Cash A/c		1,250	2010 Apr 1	By Balance c/d		1,250
			1,250				1,250
Apr 1	To Balance b/d		1,250				

Commission Account

Dr.							Cr.
Date	Particulars	J.F	Rs.	Date	Particulars	J.F	Rs.
2010 Mar 22	To Cash A/c		800	2010 Apr 1	By Balance c/d		800
			800				800
Apr 1	To Balance b/d		800				

Interest Account

Dr.							Cr.
Date	Particulars	J.F	Rs.	Date	Particulars	J.F	Rs.
2010 Mar 31	To Cash A/c		300	2010 Apr 1	By Balance c/d		300
			300				300
Apr 1	To Balance b/d		300				

ZaCo's Account

Dr.							Cr.
Date	Particulars	J.F	Rs.	Date	Particulars	J.F	Rs.
2010 Mar 1	To Balance b/d		28,000	2010 Mar 9	By Cash A/c		7,000
7	To Sales A/c		14,700	31	By Bal c/d		35,700
			42,700				42,700
Apr 1	To Balance b/d		35,700				

Capital Account

Dr.   Cr.

Date	Particulars	J.F	Rs.	Date	Particulars	J.F	Rs.
2010 Mar 31	To bal c/d		60,000	2010 Mar 1	By Balance b/d		60,000
			60,000				60,000
				Apr 1	By Balance b/d		60,000

Mr. Chandra's Account

Dr.   Cr.

Date	Particulars	J.F	Rs.	Date	Particulars	J.F	Rs.
2010 Mar 12	To Bank A/c		5,000	2010 Mar 1	By Balance b/d		9,000
31	To Balance c/d		9,700	2	By Purchase A/c		5,700
			14,700				14,700
				Apr 1	To Balance b/d		9,700

Maya's Loan Account

Dr.   Cr.

Date	Particulars	J.F	Rs.	Date	Particulars	J.F	Rs.
2010 Mar 31	To Balance c/d		30,000	2010 Apr 1	By Cash A/c		30,000
			30,000				30,000
				Apr 1	To Balance b/d		30,000

Office Equipment Account

Dr.   Cr.

Date	Particulars	J.F	Rs.	Date	Particulars	J.F	Rs.
2010 Mar 15	To Cash A/c		4,000	2010 Mar 31	By Balance c/d		4,000
			4,000				4,000
Apr	To Balance b/d		4,000				

Drawings Account

Dr.							Cr.
Date	Particulars	J.F	Rs.	Date	Particulars	J.F	Rs.
2010				2010			
Mar 17	To Cash A/c		2,500	Mar 31	By Balance c/d		12,000
26	To Bank A/c		8,500				
27	To Goods A/c (stock)		1,000				
			12,000				12,000
Apr 1			12,000				

5.7 TRIAL BALANCE

5.7.1 Introduction :

The fundament principle of double entry book keeping is that debit must be equal to credit. In other words, debit aspect of any transaction is always equal to its credit aspect.

All ledger accounts are balances. A debit balance in a general ledger account indicates an excess of debit side over credit side of the account. A credit balance in a ledger account indicates the excess of credit side over debit side of the account. A trial balance is a summary of all the ledger balances outstanding as on particular date. List of debit balances and credit balances should be equal. It said that Trial balance is tallied. When trial balance tallies is establishes the arithmetical accuracy of record. It is a statement prepared before preparing the final accounts. It is a link between books of account and final accounts i.e. the Trading & Profit & Loss A/c and Balance Sheet.

5.7.2 Types of trial balances

Trial balances are of two types.
1) Gross Trial Balance
2) Net Trial Balance

1 Gross Trial Balance :

Gross Trial Balance is prepared by taking all ledger account debit total and credit total, instead of considering ledger balances, as on a particular date.

Illustration 3 : Gross Trial Balance can be as under –

Sr. No.	Name of Account		Total debit side (Rs.)	Total credit side (Rs.)
1	Ketan's Capital		5,000	76,000
2	Opening Stock		10,000	-
3	Purchases Sales		2,10,000	2,000
4	Sales Return		2,000	3,05,000
5	Expenses		18,000	-
6	Customers		27,000	-
7	Suppliers		1,20,000	26,000
8	Cash		12,000	80,000
9	U. C. Bank		6,000	-
10			96,000	17,000
			5,06,000	**5,06,000**

2 Net Trial balance :

Net trial balance is list of debit & credit balance, taken from ledger accounts on particular date. Normally, net trial balance is prepare, since it is transferred to final accounts and personal and real accounts balance are carried forward from current year to subsequent year.

Illustration 4 : Trial Balance as on 31st March 2010.

Sr. No.	Name of Account		Total debit side (Rs.)	Total credit side (Rs.)
1	Opening Stock		12,000	-
2	Capital Purchases		-	1,02,000
3	Purchase Return		2,10,000	-
4	Sales		-	6,000
5	Sales Return		-	3,11,000
6	Expenses		4,000	-
7	Plant & Machinery		28,000	-
8	Customers		1,20,000	-
9	Suppliers		80,000	-
10	Cash		-	62,000
11	Bank balance		6,000	-
12			21,000	-
			4,81,000	**4,81,000**

1.   Capital   :   Credit balance
2.   Drawings   :   Debit balance
3.   Purchases   :   Debit balance
4.   Expenses   :   Debit balance
5.   Incomes   :   Credit balance
6.   Carriage Inwards   :   Debit balance
7.   Carriage Outwards :   Debit balance
8.   Stock (opening)   :   Debit balance
9.   Loan taken   :   Credit balance
10. Interest paid   :   Debit balance
11. Loan given   :   Debit balance
12. Interest received :   Credit balance
13. Assets   :   Debit balance
14. Suppliers   :   Credit balance
15. Sales Return   :   Debit balance
16. Purchases   :   Debit balance
17. Return Outwards   :   Credit balance
18. Investments   :   Debit balance
19. Goodwill   :   Debit balance
20. Cash   :   Debit balance

Note : Closing stock should not be taken in trial balance. However, it Gross Profit is given in trial balance then it should be taken as Debit balance.

5.9   ILLUSTRATIONS-2

Illustration 5 : From the following prepare Gross Trial balance and net Trial balance as on 31st March 2010.

Particulars	Totals
Cash (Dr.)	21,500
Bank (Dr.)	13,000
Furniture (Dr.)	21,000
Creditors (Dr.)	13,700
Debtors (Dr.)	22,000
Rent (Dr.)	5,500
Salaries (Dr.)	2,900
Cash (Cr.)	14,300

Capital (Cr.)	10,000	
Bank (Cr.)	2,900	
Furniture (Cr.)	400	
Creditors (Cr.)	14,000	
Debtor (Cr.)	4,800	
Rent (Cr.)	900	

Solution :

(A) Gross Trial Balance as on 31.03.2010

Particulars (i.e. Names of Accounts)	Debit Total (Rs.)	Credit Total (Rs.)
Cash	21,500	14,300
Bank	13,000	2,900
Furniture	21,000	400
Creditors	13,700	14,000
Debtors	22,000	4,800
Rent	5,500	900
Salaries	2,900	-
Capital	-	62,300
	99,600	**99,600**

(B) Net Trial Balance

Particulars	Debit Balance (Rs.)	Credit Balance (Rs.)
Cash (Dr. – Cr.) Bank	7,200	-
(Dr. – Cr.) Furniture	10,100	-
(Dr. – Cr.) Creditors	20,600	-
(Cr. – Dr.) Debtors	-	300
(Dr. – Cr.) Rent (Dr.	17,200	-
– Cr.) Salaries	4,600	-
Capital	2,900	-
	-	62,300
	62,600	**62,600**

Illustration 6 : Prepare a Trial Balance from the following items :

Particulars	Totals
Capital	7,63,050
Furniture & Fixture	40,000
Land & Building	4,03,000
Plant & Machinery	2,00,000
Drawings	60,000
Patents	20,000
Stock	4,00,000
Purchases	9,50,000
Wages	50,000
Salaries	72,000
Sundry Debtors	3,50,000
Sales	13,20,000
Sales Returns	61,000
Purchases Returns	10,000
Loan from Ketan Rent,	4,00,000
Rates & Taxes Bad	48,000
Debts	4,000
Sundry Creditors	2,24,000
Discount received	9,000
Trade Expenses	700
Interest on Loan	4,500
Insurance	6,500
Traveling Expenses	3,000
Cash in Hand	2,100
Cash at Bank	51,250

Solution :

Trial balance

Particulars	Debit (Rs.)	Credit (Rs.)
Capital	-	7,63,050
Furniture & Fixture	40,000	-
Land & Building	4,03,000	-
Plant & Machinery	2,00,000	-
Drawings	60,000	-
Patents	20,000	-

Stock	4,00,000	-
Purchases	9,50,000	-
Wages	50,000	-
Salaries	72,000	-
Sundry Debtors	3,50,000	-
Sales	-	13,20,000
Sales Returns	61,000	-
Purchases Returns	-	10,000
Loan from Ketan Rent,	-	4,00,000
Rates & Taxes Bad	48,000	-
Debts	4,000	-
Sundry Creditors	-	2,24,000
Discount received	-	9,000
Trade Expenses	700	-
Interest on Loan	4,500	-
Insurance	6,500	-
Traveling Expenses	3,000	-
Cash in Hand	2,100	-
Cash at Bank	51,250	-
	27,26,050	27,26,050

5.10 EXERCISES :

5.10.1 Theory questions :

1. What is ledger?

2. How entries from Journal posted to Ledger?

3. Why Real Account have always debit balance or nil balance.

4. What are different types of Trial Balance?

5. Why Trial Balance tallies?

6. Distinguish between Gross Trial Balance and Net Trial Balance.

7. Why Trial Balance prepared?

5.10.2 Practical Problems :

Q.1 Prepare a Trial balance from the following as on March 31st, 2010.

Particulars	Totals
Stock	60,000
Purchases	1,50,000
Capital	70,000
Drawings	22,000
Sales	2,50,000
Traveling Expenses	1,320
Salaries	11,200
Rent, Taxes & Insurance	5,600
Returns Outwards	2,600
Advertising	840
Wages	7,000
Bank Overdraft	20,000
General Trade Expenses	1,350
Returns Inwards	5,400
Discount allowed	600
Interest & Commission paid	430
Bad Debts Sundry	800
Creditors Cash in	60,000
hand Sundry	2,060
Debtors Furniture	92,000
Plant & Machinery	10,000
Buildings	20,000
	12,000

Q.2 Following are the balances extracted from the ledger of Shri. Ketan. Prepare a Trial Balance as on 31st Dec. 2010.

Particulars	Rs.	Particulars	Rs.
Capital A/c	40,000	Purchases	26,500
Drawings A/c	4,000	Printing & Stationery	3,000
Sundry Creditors	18,440	Rent & Taxes	2,500
Motor Car Expenses	3,000	Office Expenses	7,000
Sales	29,560	Commission paid	5,000
Trade Expenses	8,500	Sundry Debtors	18,000
Insurance	1,030	Discount Allowed	2,970
Opening Stock	8,500	Interest Received	2,000

Q.3 The following balances appeared in the ledger of M/s. Tata Traders as on 1st July 2010.

Debit Balance	Rs.	Credit Balance	Rs.
Cash A/c	35,000	Capital A/c	80,000
Bank A/c	30,000	Kamath"s A/c	5,000
Goods A/c	35,000	10% Term Loan	20,000
Mehta"s & Son"s A/c	15,000		
	1,05,000		1,05,000

2010

July 1 Borrowed Rs.25,000/- from wife for expansion of the business and deposited Rs.20,000/- in Bank.

4 Deposited Rs.15,000/- into the Bank.

6 Received from Mr. Mehta and Sons Rs.9,550/- in part payment of Rs.10,000/-.

8 Paid Rs.1,900/- to Mr. Kamath in part payment of Rs.2,000/-.

20 Withdrew from bank Rs.5,000/- for office use and Rs.4,000/- for private use.

24 Cash sales Rs.20,000/-.

25 Paid Salaries Rs.1,250/-, rent Rs.1,400/- and received commission Rs.2,600/- in cash.

28 Paid Rs.20,000/- for part payment of wife"s loan. Also interest of Rs.1,250/- due on loan.

31 Deposited Rs.11,500/- into the Bank.

From the above transactions, draft journal entries, post them to respective ledger accounts and balance them, also prepare Trial Balance.

❑❑❑❑❑

Unit - 6

FINAL ACCOUNTS OF A SOLE TRADER

Unit Structure:

6.0   OBJECTIVES

After studying the unit the students will be able to:

- Know the meaning of Final Accounts and proforma of Final Accounts.

- Explain the Classification of Assets and Liabilities. •

Make the adjustment entries.

- Prepare Final Accounts from the given Trial Balance.

6.1   INTRODUCTION

The transactions of a business are first recorded in Journal / subsidiary books, then posted there form to the Ledger and at the end of accounting year, Trial balance is prepare to test accuracy, both the aspects of the transactions have been correctly recorded in the books of accounts of original entry as well as in the Ledger. The last stage in accounting process is the preparation of final Accounts.

From given trial balance a Trading, Profit & Loss A/c & Balance Sheet is prepared.

A Trading, Profit & Loss A/c is prepared to determine the Profit or Loss made during a particular year, and Balance Sheet is prepare which consists of all assets, Liabilities and Capital of proprietor.

For preparing Final Accounts from Trial Balance following procedure should be followed.

i) Debit Account balances :-

Balances appearing on the debit column of the trial balance may represent - (a) assets (b) Expenses and Losses. Assets are shown on right hand side of the balance sheet while expenses and loss are debited either to the Trading A/c or to the Profit & Loss A/c, depending upon nature of expenditure or loss.

ii) Credit Account balances :-

Credit items in the trial balance represents (a) Capital, Liabilities, expenses. These items are entered on the left hand side of the balance sheet (b) Income and gains. These are either credited to Trading A/c or Profit and Loss A/c.

6.2 TRADING ACCOUNT :-

Trading A/c is prepared to ascertain the Gross Profit. Gross Profit is difference between net sales and cost of goods sold. A specimen of Trading Account is given below:

Trading A/c for the year ended...

Dr.   Cr.

Particulars	Rs.	Particulars	Rs.
To Opening Stock	X	By Sales X	X
To Purchases X		Less: Returns (X)	
Less: Returns (X)	X	By Closing Stock	X
To Carriage Inwards	X		
To Wages	X		
To Direct Expenses	X		
To Gross Profit	X		
	XX		XX

However, Gross Profit is the balancing figure, in case debit side total exceeds the credit side, then balance will be Gross Loss, it is shown on credit side of Trading A/c as „By Gross Loss".

6.3   PROFIT AND LOSS ACCOUNT

Profit and Loss A/c is prepared to calculate the net profit or net loss. The balance of Trading A/c i.e. Gross profit / Gross loss is transferred to the Profit and Loss Account.   Therefore,   all   those expenses and Losses are debited to the Profit and Loss A/c. Other income / gains are credited to this A/c e.g. commission received, discount earn etc.

The   Profit   and   Loss   accounts   measures   net   profit   by matching   revenues   and   expenses   according   to   the   accounting principles, Net profit is the excess of revenue over total expenses. It should be kept in mind that all expenses / incomes must be adjusted in respect of outstanding / prepaid / paid or received in advance.

Expenses or incomes are considered on mercantile basis. At end Net Profit or Net Loss transferred to Capital Account in the balance sheet.

A specimen of Profit & Loss Account is given below :

Profit & Loss Account for the year ended...

Dr.   Cr.

Particulars	Rs.	Particulars	Rs.
To Salaries	X	By Gross Profit b/d	X
To Rent, Rates & Taxes	X	By Discount earned	X
To Insurance	X	By Commission received	X
To Printing & Stationery	X	By Interest earned	X
To Legal Exp	X	By Profit on sale of assets	X
To Audit Fees	X		
To Discount allowed	X		
To Interest paid on Loans	X		
To Bad debts	X		
To Carriage outwards	X		
To Advertising expenses	X		
To Depreciation on assets	X		
To Loss due to fire	X		
To Net Profit [transferred to capital]	X		
	XX		XX

It may be noted that:

1) Direct Expenses which are debited to Trading A/c are not debited again to Profit & loss A/c.

2) Personal expenses are not debited to this account.

3) Income Tax, Wealth Tax or Life insurance premium paid are personal expenses of proprietor / partners.

4) Items shown in Trial Balance should be given one effect and adjustment given below Trial Balance should be given two effects.

5) It should be noted that:

Trading Account and Profit & Loss Account are not prepares separately as shown above but they are prepared as one account split up into two sections.   As such the combined heading is given as „Trading and Profit & Loss A/c for the year ended…"

6.4   BALANCE SHEET

Balance Sheet is a statement which shows the financial position of a business entity on a given date. It is prepared from trial balance, after all nominal accounts and accounts relating to Trading, Profit & Loss account. Accounts left out are Real accounts and personal accounts.   Accounts   having   debit   balances transferred to Assets side of balance sheet and account having credit balance transferred to Liabilities side of Balance Sheet, in some cases credit balances may be deducted from particular asset. e.g. provision for depreciation deducted from Fixed Asset; Reserve for bad & doubtful, is deducted from sundry debtors. Balances shown in Balance Sheets are carried forward for next year.

The Balance Sheet has also two sides. The Left hand side is headed as „Liabilities" and Right hand side is headed as „Assets". It is not an account, therefore in no „To" or „By" proceeding the names of the Account recorded in the Balance Sheet.

Balance Sheet shows financial position as on a particular date and not for the year. Therefore the heading of Balance Sheet is worded as "Balance Sheet of ….. as on ….."

6.5   MARSHALLING OF BALANCE SHEET

[Order of Assets and Liabilities]

1) Assets are arranged in order of their Liquidity i.e. in order in which they can be converted into cash and Liabilities they are payable.   As assets which can be immediately converted into cash will be taken first and then in order will follow the others. Similarly, Liability which is to be paid off immediately will be taken first and then next and so on.

2) The assets & liabilities are arranged in exactly the reverse order of the above arrangement.

A specimen of Balance Sheet is given below :

Balance Sheet of ….. as on …..
[According to Liquidity order]

Liabilities	Rs.	Assets	Rs.
Outstanding Expenses	X	Cash in hand	X
Sundry Creditors	X	Bank Balance	X
Bills Payable	X	Investments	X
Bank Overdrafts	X	Sundry Debtors	X
Loans	X	Bills Receivable	X
Capital	X	Outstanding Income	X
		Stock in trade	X
		Loose tools	X
		Prepaid Expenses	X
		Patents, Trade Marks	X
		Furniture	X
		Plant & Machinery	X
		Building	X
		Land	X
		Goodwil	X
	XXX		**XXX**

The totals of the two sides of the balance sheet must agree because of the equation

$$Assets = Liabilities + Capital$$

6.6   CLASSIFICATION OF ASSETS

6.6.1 Fixed Assets :-

These assets are acquired for long use in the business itself and not for sale. e.g. Building, Plant & Machinery etc.

6.6.2 Current or Floating Assets :-

These assets are to be converted into cash as soon as possible. e.g. stock of goods, Sundry Debtors, Bills Receivable.

6.6.3 Liquid / Quick Assets :-

These assets can be converted into cash as quickly as possible, without undue Loss. e.g. Sundry Debtors, Bank Balance, short term govt. securities.

6.6.4 Wasting Assets :-

Are those fixed assets which have fixed content like coal in coal mine.

6.6.5 Intangible Assets :-

Are those Fixed Assets which can not be seen or touched or felt, i.e. having no physical existence, e.g. Goodwill.

6.6.6 Fictitious Assets :-

Are worthless assets but shown as assets in the Balance Sheet. E.g. preliminary expenses, Discount on issue of debentures.

6.7 CLASSIFICATION OF LIABILITIES

6.7.1 Fixed and Long-term Liabilities :-

Are those Liabilities which are payable after a long period of time e.g. Bank Loan, Debentures.

6.7.2 Current Liabilities :-

These are short term Liabilities payable usually with in year e.g. sundry creditors, Bills Payable, outstanding expenses.

6.7.3 Contingent Liabilities :-

These are not actual Liabilities as on date of Balance Sheet, which may or may not be payable in future, depend on the happening of certain events. In future, however due present circumstances; whether to pay or not, depends upon further happenings. Therefore existence of contingent liabilities shown below total liabilities by way of note for the sake of information and disclosure. e.g. investment in partly paid shares, compensation suit pending in court, Bills discounting but not matured, such Liabilities are shown as a foot note in the Balance Sheet on liabilities side.

6.8 LIMITATIONS OF BALANCE SHEET

- Balance sheet is considered to be a static document. The real position of the concern keeps on changing.

- Stock valuation / method of depreciation are different, which affects on financial position.

- Change in accounting policy may not followed consistally.

- Window-dressing is accomplished in general ways, e.g. not making adequate provisions.

- Fixed assets are shown at historical cost less depreciation. However, actual value of fixed assets, like Land might have appreciated much more.

6.9 ADJUSTMENTS

Before an accountant can proceeds to prepare the Final Accounts from trial balance, he has to process some additional information, which is not consider in trial balance.

The following are a few examples showing where adjustment entries would required :

1 Closing Stock / Inventory :-

Unsold goods in stock at the end of the period. Closing stock is valued at cost or market value which ever is lower. For accounting following entry is pass

Closing Stock A/c.........................Dr   XX
          To Trading A/c   XX

While closing stock appears on credit side of Trading A/c and it also appears on an assets, in the Balance Sheet.

2 Outstanding Expenses :-

The nominal accounts records the actual expenses paid during the period, However some expenses are incurred, (due) but not paid, hence it is not accounted, are also brought into the books to help in proper matching of revenues and expenses.   e.g. Firm pays wages on 10th of the subsequent mouth. These for at the end of the year say 31st march "10, wages account is debited up to Feb. 10; since March wage not paid.   These unpaid / outstanding expenses must also be included. This is done by passing following adjustment entry.

```
Wages A/c.............................Dr  XX
        To outstanding wages A/c              XX
```

The above entries increases wages in Trading A/c and it is since not paid shown a Liability in the balance sheet.

3   Prepaid Expenses :-

Certain expenses paid may relate to more than one accounting period.   It is necessary to ascertain that portion of expense which the benefit is not yet received by the concern. e.g. In such premium paid Rs. 6000, for the year ended 31st march 2010. Prepare Final Accounts for the ended 31st Dec 2009. Hence Jan to March, three month insurance premium benefit to the subsequent three month.   Such expenses paid in a advance are called „pre-paid expenses". Adjustment entry pass as under :

```
Prepaid Expenses A/c..................Dr  XX
        To Expenses A/c                        XX
```

Prepaid expenses deducted from concern period and shown in the balance sheet an assets.

4   Depreciation :-

It is the reduction or fall in the value of a Fixed Assets due to its use.   Thus, the depreciation is loss to the business, to account for following adjustment entry is passed.

```
Depreciation A/c.........................Dr  XX
        To Fixed Assets A/c                    XX
```

Depreciation is debited to Profit & Loss A/c and it is deducted from concerned Fixed Assets in the Balance Sheet.

5   Outstanding / Accrued Income :-

Income earned during the period but not received, Entry-

```
Outstanding Income A/c.................Dr  XX
        To Income A/c                          XX
```

It added to Income in Profit & Loss A/c and shown as assets in the Balance Sheet.

6   Income Received in Advance :-

Entry-
Income received, however it relate to subsequent year;

Income A/c…………………………....Dr XX
To Income Received in Advance A/c   XX

Advance income deducted from income on credit side of Profit & Loss A/c and shown it on Liability side of Balance Sheet.

7   Bad debts :-

When goods are sold on credit the amount is recoverable from customer. However amount receivable is not possible to recover, then such debts is to be written off, as Loss to business; Entry-

Bad debts A/c………………………...Dr   XX
To Customer A/c   XX

It is debited to Profit & Loss A/c as bad debts and deducted from sundry Debtors in the balance sheet.

These are money adjustment, however, only few basis adjustment discuss above:

8   Hidden Adjustment in Trial Balance :-

These adjustments not directly however from Trial Balance, these are apparent, and hence must be consider.

	Trial Balance On 31-03-2010	Trading, Profit & Loss A/c	Balance Sheet
1.	Rent paid (Including Rs.400/- for April)	Deduct Rs.400/- from Rent Paid A/c	Show Rs.400/- as Rent Prepaid on Assets side
2.	Rent paid (upto Feb.) Rs.2,200/-	Add Rs.200/- to Rent Paid A/c	Show Rs.200/- as O/S Rent on Liability side
3.	Rent Received (upto Feb.)	Add Rs.300/- to Rent Received A/c	Show Rs.300/- as Rent Due on Assets side
4.	Rent Received (incl. Rs.500/- for April)	Deduct Rs.500/- from Rent Received A/c	Show Rs.500/- as Advance Rent on Liability side
5.	Leasehold Land : Rs.1,00,000/- (for 10 years from 01-04-2010)	Write off Rs.10,000/- on Dr. side	Deduct Rs.10,000/- form Leasehold Land on Assets side
6.	(a) Loan from ABC Rs.20,000/- (b) Interest to 10% p.a. Rs.1,500/-	Add Rs.500/- to Interest Paid A/c	Show Rs.500/- as Interest Due on Liabilities side
7.	(a) Machinery (W.D.V.) : Rs.7,500/- (b) Machinery sold for Rs.9,000/-	Show Profit Rs.1,500/- on Cr. side	Deduct Rs.7,500/- from Machinery A/c in Balance Sheet

CHECK YOUR PROGRESS

- Give the effects of the following adjustments:

    1. Salary Rs. 4000 is Outstanding.

    2. Prepaid rent Rs.1000.

    3. Wages included Rs.4000 which is used for installation of Machinery.

    4. Interest on Investment Rs.3000 received in advance.

6.10 ILLUSTRATIONS

Illustration 1:

From the following Trial Balance of Shri - Atul Sheth prepare Trading and Profit and Loss A/c for the year ended 31st March, 2010 and a Balance Sheet on that date.

Trial Balance as on 31st March, 2010

Particulars	Dr. Rs.	Cr. Rs.
Machinery	90,000	
Building	50,000	
Stock (01-04-09)	10,200	
Purchases	80,800	
Wages & Salaries	17,000	
Carriage Outwards	3,000	
Sundry Debtors	50,000	
General expenses	9,100	
Rent	1,700	
Bad Debts	650	
Income Tax	600	
Legal Charges	800	
Atul Sheth"s Drawing	18,000	
Cash In hand	24,000	
Cash at bank	18,000	1,20,200
Atul Sheth"s		18,000
Capital Sundry		23,000
Creditors Bills		1,800
Payable Returns		3,300
Outwards Interest		2,07,550
Sales		
	3,73,850	3,73,850

Adjustments :-

The following adjustments should be taken into consideration :-

1) Stock on 31st March,2010 was Rs.70,000/- valued at cost and market price Rs.82,000/-.

2) Depreciate Machinery at 10% and Building @ 5%.

3) Rent Outstanding Rs.800/-.

91

Solution :-

Shri Atul Sheth's

Trading and Profit & Loss Account for the year ended as on 31st March 2010

Dr.   Cr.

Particulars	Rs.	Particulars	Rs.
To Opening Stock	10,200	By Sales	2,07,550
To Purchases 80,800		By Closing Stock	70,000
(-) P. Return 1,800	79,000		
To Wage and Salaries	17,000		
To Gross Profit c/d	1,71,350		
	2,77,550		2,77,550
To Carriage Outward	3,000	By Gross Profit b/d	1,71,350
To General Expenses	9,100	By Interest	3,300
To Rent 1,700			
(+) Outstanding 800	2,500		
To Bad Debts	650		
To Legal Charges	800		
To Depreciation			
On Machinery	9,000		
On Building	2,500		
To Net Profit c/d	1,47,100		
	1,74,650		1,74,650

Shri Atul Sheth's
Balance sheet as on 31/03/2010

Liabilities	Rs.	Rs.	Assets	Rs.	Rs.
Capital balance	1,20,200		Machinery	90,000	
(+) Net Profit	1,47,100		(-)	(9,000)	81,000
(-) Drawings	(18,000)		Depreciation	50,000	
(-) Income Tax	(600)	2,48,700	Building	(2,500)	47,500
Sundry		18,000	(-)		50,000
Creditors Bills		23,000	Depreciation		24,000
Payable		800	Sundry		18,000
			Debtors Cash		70,000
		2,90,500			2,90,500

Illustration 2:

From the following Trial balance extracted from the books of Shri Sunit as on 31st December 2009. Prepare his final accounts as on 31st December 2009 after taking into consideration following adjustments.

Trial balance as on Dec. 31, 2009

Particulars	Dr. Rs.	Cr. Rs.
Sundry Creditors		28,000
Rent	5,000	
Cash at Bank	42,000	
Cash in hand	28,000	
Stock as on 1 Jan. 2009	18,000	
Bad debts	900	
Discounts	1,800	1,200
Purchase and Sales	65,000	1,08,000
Carriage on Sales	3,500	
Plant and Machinery	48,000	
Sales Return	1,200	1,800
Purchase Return		
Carriage on Purchases	7,500	
Furniture and Fixtures	80,000	
Insurance	8,000	
Salaries	9,000	
Bills Receivable	18,000	

Wages		6,000			
Capital				3,50,000	
Sundry Debtors		1,20,900			
Commission		4,200			
		4,89,000		**4,89,000**	

Adjustments –

1) Depreciate Plant and Machinery 10%.

2) Insurance prepaid Rs.1,500/-.

3) Outstanding Salaries Rs.1,200/-.

4) Closing Stock Rs.81,000/-.

Solution :

Shri Sunit's Final Accounts
Trading and Profit and Loss Account for the year ended as on 31st December 2009

Dr.   Cr.

Particulars	Rs.	Rs.	Particulars	Rs.	Rs.
To Opening Stock		18,000	By Sales	1,08,000	
To Purchases	65,000		(-) Sales Return		1,06,800
(-) Purchase Return		63,200	By Closing Stock		81,000
To Carriage on		7,500			
Purchases		6,000			
To Wages		93,100			
		1,87,800			1,87,800
To Rent		5,000	By Gross Profit b/d		93,100
To Insurance	8,000				1,200
(-) Prepaid		6,500	By Discount		
To Bad		900			
Debts To		1,800			
Discount To	9,000				
Salaries		10,200			
(+) Outstanding		3,500			
To Carriage on		4,200			
Sales					
To Commission		4,800			
To Depreciation		57,400			
on					
		94,300			**94,300**

94

Shri Sunit's
Balance Sheet as on 31st December 2009

Liabilities	Rs.	Rs.	Assets	Rs.	Rs.
Capital balance	3,50,000		Plant & Mach.	48,000	
(+) Net Profit (-)	57,400		(-)	(4,800)	43,200
Drawings	(22,000)	3,85,400	Depreciation		42,000
Sundry		28,000	Cash at Bank		28,000
Creditors O/s		1,200	Cash in hand		
Salaries			Furniture &		80,000
			Fixtures		1,20,900
			Sundry		81,000
			Debtors		
			Closing Stock		1,500
			Prepaid		18,000
		4,14,600			4,14,600

Illustration 3:

From the following Trial Balance and additional information prepare Profit and Loss Account for the year ended 31/03/2008 and Balance Sheet as on that date of Shri Ankur.

Trial Balance as on 31/03/2008

Particulars	Dr. Rs.	Cr. Rs.
Sundry Debtors	88,000	
Capital		3,16,300
Salaries	9,000	
Commission	800	
Furniture	90,000	
Creditors		81,000
Dividend		4,000
Machinery	1,56,000	
Bad debts	2,250	
Advertisement	1,000	
Investments	38,000	
Bills Payable		18,000
Opening Stock (01/04/07)	32,000	
Insurance	11,000	
Drawings	17,000	
Cash in hand	35,000	

Particulars	Rs.	Rs.
Interest		900
Purchases	1,34,500	
Sales Returns	1,800	
Wages	6,500	
Bills Receivable	32,000	
Purchase Return		2,300
Sales		2,10,000
Carriage Inward	2,100	
Octroi	1,500	
Bank Overdraft		76,950
	7,09,450	7,09,450

Adjustments –

1) Closing Stock Rs.33,000/-.

2) Wages Outstanding Rs.2,000/-.

3) Insurance prepaid Rs.2,500/-.

4) Depreciate Machinery at the rate of 10% and Furniture 15%.

Solution :

Shri Ankur's Final Account
Trading Account for the year ended 31st March 2008

Dr.   Cr.

Particulars	Rs.	Rs.	Particulars	Rs.	Rs.
To Opening Stock		32,000	By Sales	2,10,00 0	
To Purchases	1,34,50 0		(-) Sales Return		2,08,200
(-) Purchase Return	6,500	1,32,200	By Closing Stock		33,000
To Wages	2,000	8,500			
(+) Outstanding		2,100			
To Carriage Inward		1,500			
To Octroi		64,900			
		2,41,200			2,41,200

Profit and Loss Account for the year ended 31st March 2008

Dr.   Cr.

Particulars	Rs.	Rs.	Particulars	Rs.	Rs.
To Insurance	11,000		By Gross Profit		64,900
(-) Prepaid	2,500	8,500	By Dividend		4,000
To Salaries		9,000	By Interest		900
To Commission		800			
To Bad Debts		2,250			
To Advertisement		1,000			
To					
Depreciation		15,600			
On		4,500			
Machinery		28,150			
On Furniture					
		69,800			69,800

Balance sheet as on 31st March, 2008

Liabilities	Rs.	Rs.	Assets	Rs.	Rs.
Capital balance	3,16,300		Machinery	1,56,000	
(+) Net	28,150		(-) Dep^n 10%	(15,600)	1,40,400
Profit (-)	(17,000)	3,27,450	Sundry Debtors		88,000
Drawings		2,000	Bills Receivable		32,000
O/s Wages		81,000	Closing Stock		33,000
Creditors		18,000	Prepaid Insurance		2,500
Bills		76,950	Furniture	90,000	
Payable			(-) Dep^n 5%	(4,500)	85,500
Bank Overdraft			Investments		38,000
			Cash in hand		35,000
			Cash at Bank		51,000
		5,05,400			5,05,400

6.11 EXERCISES

6.11.1 Theory Questions

1) Explain what is Final Account?

2) Distinguish between Trial balance and Balance sheet

3) Write short notes on a)

Adjustment

b) Outstanding Expenses c)

Gross Profit

d) Prepaid Expenses e)

Fixed Assets

f) Floating Assets

4) What are the limitations of Balance Sheet.

6.11.2 Practical Problems

Q.1 Below is the trial balance of Suresh as at 31st March, 2010

Debit balance	Rs.	Credit balance	Rs.
Suresh"s Current A/c	1,500	Capital Account	50,000
Purchases	7,60,450	Loan from Mohan @ 9%	20,000
Salaries	4,200	(taken on 1st October	
Carriage on Purchases	400	09) Sales	7,20,000
Carriage on Sale	500	Discount	500
Lighting	300	Sundry Debtors	20,000
Rates and Insurance	400		
Buildings	27,000		
Sundry Debtors	8,000		
Furniture	6,000		
Cash in hand	250		
Cash at bank	1,500		
	8,10,500		8,10,500

Rates have been prepaid to the extent of Rs.175/-, Bad debts totaling Rs.500/- have to be written off. Buildings have to be depreciated at 2% and Furniture @ 10%.

You are required to prepare the Profit and Loss Account for the year ended 31st March, 2010 and the balance sheet as on that date.

Q.2 From the following prepare Trading Account Profit and Loss Account and Balance Sheet.

Trial Balance as 31st March, 2011

Sr. No.	Name of the Account	L.F.	Debit (Rs.)	Credit (Rs.)
1	Sundry Debtors		15,000	-
2	Buildings		40,000	-
3	Goodwill		30,000	-
4	Bills Payable		-	45,000
5	Sundry Creditors		-	25,000
6	Plant & Machinery		1,60,000	-
7	Opening Stock		35,000	-
8	Sales		-	1,40,000
9	Bank Overdraft		-	1,25,000
10	Bills Receivable		40,000	-
11	Purchases		1,25,000	-
12	Sales Returns		1,000	-
13	Wages		45,000	-
14	Purchase Returns		-	1,500
15	Carriage Inwards		600	-
16	Carriage Outwards		300	-
17	Office Salaries		12,000	-
18	Office Rent		500	-
19	Commission		600	-
20	Postage & Telegram		100	-
21	Depreciation		500	-
22	Printing & Stationery		45	-
23	Bad Debts		200	-
24	Prepaid Insurance		150	-
25	Cash in hand Cash		6,000	-
26	at Bank Income		9,000	-
27	Receivable Capital		400	-
28	Account Drawings		-	1,90,000
29			5,105	-
			5,26,500	**5,26,500**

Closing stock valued at Rs.1,10,000/-.

Q.3 Prepare Trading and Profit and Loss Account from the following trial balance and adjustments for the year ending 31st December, 2008. Prepare Balance sheet as at that date.

Trial balance as on 31st December, 2008

Name of the Account	L.F.	Debit (Rs.)	Credit (Rs.)
Capital Account		-	2,00,000
Drawings Account		86,000	-
Stock (01/01/2008)		75,000	-
Bills Receivable		15,000	-
Sales		-	1,62,350
Purchases		50,000	-
Returns		2,000	3,000
Salaries & Wages		12,000	-
Creditors		-	15,000
Insurance Carriage		3,500	-
Inwards Carriage		1,500	-
Outwards Debtors		850	-
Commission		68,000	-
Interest		3,000	2,000
Discount		4,500	3,000
Bills Payable		3,500	3,000
Printing & Stationery		-	12,000
Trade Expenses		2,500	-
Furniture & Fixtures		1,500	-
Cash in hand		11,000	-
Cash at bank		46,000	-
Rent & taxes		12,000	-
		2,500	-
		4,00,350	**4,00,350**

Adjustments –

1) Closing Stock was valued at Rs.1,05,000/-.

2) Furniture valued at Rs.10,000/-.

3) Outstanding Expenses : Salaries at 1,200/-, Rent & Taxes Rs.600/- and prepaid insurance Rs.650/-.

Unit - -7

PARTNERSHIP FINAL ACCOUNTS

Unit Structure:

7.0   OBJECTIVES

After studying the Unit the students will be able to:

- Define partnership and explain the characteristics of Partnership.

- Explain the types of Partners.

- Understand the methods of maintaining Capital accounts

- Make the adjustment entries and prepare the Final accounts of a partnership firm.

7.1   INTRODUCTION

In small business, sole trader can manage business. He can himself provide the capital and supervise the work. However, there are numbers of limitations : To over come limitations, businessmen may convert his business into Partnership. Each partner contribute capital and in return each partner get a share in the profits of the firm.

7.2   DEFINITION :

As per Indian Partnership Act 1932, "Partnership is the relation between persons who have agreed to share the Profit / Loss of a business carried on by all or any of them acting for all."

7.3 CHARACTERISTICS OF PARTNERSHIP

a) It is a voluntary association of persons.

b) The relations among them are contractual.

c) Each partner is <u>Principal</u> as well as <u>Agent</u>.

d) All the partners can take active part in business.

e) Profit / Loss are shared by the partners as per Partnership Deed.

f) Minimum two and maximum 10 partners are allowed for banking business, however maximum 20 partners are all for the general business.

g) The liability of the partners is unlimited.

7.4 TYPES OF PARTNERS

i)	Active Partner	: taking active part in firm business
ii)	Sleeping / Dormant Partner	: Not taking active part in business, provides capital.
iii)	Nominal Partner	: Only he lends his name in firm.
iv)	Partners by holding / by Estoppel	: He represents himself as partner, out even though he is not a partner.
v)	Minor Partner	: He is less than 18 year old, shares in only Profit of business.
vi)	Limited Partner	: His liabilities is limited to the extent, the capital contributed by him.

7.5 PARTNERSHIP DEED

It is much agreement, in writing between the partners of the firm. The terms of contracts are written in Deed. It is prepared on stamp paper and signed by all partners. Copy partnership deed are submitted to the Bank, Income Tax Departments, Sales Tax Departments etc. Deed indicates the rights, duties and liabilities of the partner. Partnership Deed contents various term, conditions, valuation of Goodwill etc.

7.6 PROVISION OF PARTNERSHIP ACT 1932

Normally all terms and condition are stated in Partnership Deed. In case of deed is silent on certain matters, provision of Partnership Act, 1932 are applicable;

1. Profit and Losses shares by all partners equally.

2. No interest on capital and drawings.

3. No salary commission etc. payable to partner.

4. Interest @ 6% p.a. can be paid on Loan from partner.

5. Every partner can take active part in the Partnership business and can inspect the books of accounts.

6. Partner cannot start any parallel business in competition.

7.7 METHODS OF MAINTAINING CAPITAL ACCOUNT

There are two methods of maintaining Partner"s Capital Accounts.

a) Fixed Capital Method

b) Fluctuating Capital Method

7.7.1 Fixed Capital Method :

Under this method, capital contributed by partners remain fixed forever. Capital balances are not changed. Partners Current Account are open for recording transactions like interest on capital, drawing in cash or kind, share in Profit or Loss etc. Therefore Partners Current Account may have debit balance or credit balance. Debit balances of Current Account are shown on assets side of the Balance Sheet and vice versa.

7.7.2 Fluctuating Capital Method :

Under this method Capital Account of partner always fluctuates. It do not remains fixed as internal transactions of partner with firm are recorded in Capital Account only. Due to recording of internal transactions, capital balance fluctuates / changes.

7.8 PARTNERSHIP FINAL ACCOUNTS

Partnership Final Accounts consist of :
i) Trading Account
ii) Profit & Loss Account
iii) Profit and Loss Appropriation A/c
iv) Balance Sheet of Firm

7.8.1 Trading, Profit & Loss Account

Partnership Trading, Profit and Loss A/c are prepared on same line as Sole Proprietor. As these are discuss earlier, so not explain again.

7.8.2 Profit & Loss Appropriation Account

Net Profit or Net Loss from business is ascertain in Profit & Loss Account. This Net Profit / Net Loss transferred to Profit & Loss Appropriation A/c. Internal amount payable to partners like partner Salaries, Commission, Interest on Partners Capital, Interest on drawings etc. are charges against Net Profit. Balance Net Profit

/ Net Loss is transferred to Partners Current Account / Capital Account as the case may be, specimen of Profit & Loss Appropriation is as under –

Profit & Loss Appropriation Account for the year ended _____

Dr.   Cr.

Particulars	Rs.	Particulars	Rs.
To Partner's Salaries A/c	XX	By Net Profit (transferred from Profit and Loss A/c)	XX
To Partner's Commission A/c	XX	By Interest on Drawings A/c	XX
To Interest on Partners Capital A/c	XX		
To Interest on Partner's Loan A/c	XX		
To Transferred to Reserves A/c	XX		
To Net Profit transferred to partners Capital A/c (in their Profit sharing ratio)	XX		
A XX			
B XX	XX		
	XX		**XX**

7.8.3 Balance Sheet of Partnership Firm :

Balance Sheet of Partnership Firm is also like a Balance Sheet of Sole Proprietor only differ is that instead of sole proprietor capital alone, there will be each partners capital balances, may have Partners Current Account balances, Specimen of Balance Sheet as under.

Balance Sheet as on _____

Liabilities		Rs.	Assets	Rs.
Partner"sCapital A/c			Cash on hand Bank	XX
R	XX		balance Sundry	XX
K	XX		Debtors Bills	XX
G	XX	XX	Receivable Prepaid	XX
Partners Current A/c			Expenses Income	XX
R	XX		receivable	XX
G	XX	XX	Investments	XX
Sundry Creditors		XX	Office Equipments	XX
Bank Loan		XX	Plant & Machinery	XX
Outstanding Expenses		XX	Patents	XX
Income received in advance		XX	Land & Building	XX
Provident Fund		XX	Goodwill	XX
Reserve Fund		XX	Partners Current A/c	
			K XX	XX
		XX		**XX**

Balance Sheets Liabilities side total must be equal to total Assets.

7.9   ADJUSTMENTS

In addition to normal adjusts discuss in Final Accounts of Sold Trader, there may few more adjustment in respects of firm as under.

7.9.1 Interest on Capital :

Calculate interest on Capital @ rate given,

Profit & Loss Appropriation A/c .... Dr. XX

 To Interest on Partners Capital A/c   XX
(Being interest on partners" capital provided.)

Interest on Capital A/c .... Dr.   XX
        To Partner Capital A/c   XX
(Being interest on Capital transferred.)

7.9.2 Interest on Partners drawings :

Interest may be charged on drawings made by Partner to make distribution of Profit more equitable. Since drawing are made through the year it is calculated as under –If amount are withdrawn equally every month.

a) Middle of each month = Int. for 6 months

b) On 1st Day of month = Int. for 6½ month

c) On Last Day of month = Int. for 5½ month

Entry :

a) Interest on drawing A/c .... Dr.   XX
      To Profit & Loss Appropriation A/c   XX

b) Partners Capital A/c .... Dr.   XX
      To Interest on drawings A/c   XX

7.9.3 Salaries to Partners :

Profit & Loss Appropriation A/c .... Dr.   XX
      To Partner"s Capital A/c   XX

Remaining balance in Profit & Loss Appropriation Account indicates distributable Profit / Loss which should be transferred to Partner"s Capital Account.

In case of Profit

Profit & Loss Appropriation A/c .... Dr.   XX
      To A"s Capital A/c   XX
      To B"s Capital A/c   XX
(Being Net Profit transferred to partners in their Profit / Loss sharing ratio.)

Note : 1) If Partners Capital are fixed, then instead of Capital Account, all above i.e. Interest, Salary, Net Profit etc. are transferred to Partner"s Current Account.

2) Profit adjustment due to Guarantee etc. are not specially covered in syllabus & hence not considered.

7.10 LIMITED LIABILITY PARTNERSHIP ACT (L.L.P.)

The Act called Limited Liability Partnership Act (L.L.P.) extended scope and working of Partnership. A present partnership firm can also be converted into L.L.P. It has number of advantages over Partnership Firm or Private Ltd. Company. Number of partners limits not applicable to L.L.P. Here are number of advantages over Partnership Firm mainly liabilities of partners rusticated to capital contribution by partners. L.L.P. enjoys more or less advantages like in private limited company.

7.11 ILLUSTRATIONS

Illustrations 1: From the following trial balance of Neela and Sheela. You are required to prepare Trading and Profit & Loss Account for the year ended 31st March 2007 and Balance sheet as on that date after considering the following adjustments.

Trial Balance as on 31st March 2007

Particulars	Rs.	Rs.
Opening Stock	17,500	-
Salaries and Wages	4,600	-
Cash in hand	6,000	-
Purchase and Sales	1,12,600	2,65,000
Office Expenses	4,300	-
Productive Wages	7,000	-
Bills Receivable	4,000	-
Legal Expenses	3,300	-
Bad debts	1,900	-
Works Managers Salary	5,600	-
Commission Investments	1,800	2,500
Debtors	42,000	-
Creditors	67,500	-
Bank overdraft	-	92,000
Patents	-	88,000
Loose Tools	38,000	-
Furniture	28,000	-
Goodwill	65,000	-
Interest	80,000	-
Land & Building	-	1,600
Capital Accounts :	1,25,000	-
Neela		
Sheela	-	1,10,000
Drawings :	-	1,05,000
Neela	20,000	-
Sheela	30,000	-
	6,64,100	**6,64,100**

Adjustments :

1) Partners shares Profit and losses equally.

2) The Closing Stock cost Rs.25,000/- market value Rs.19,000/-.

3) Neela has withdrawn goods worth Rs.800/- for personal use.

4) Depreciate Land and Building at 10% p.a. and Loose Tools 15% p.a.

Trading Account for the year ended 31st March 2007

Particulars	Rs.	Particulars	Rs.
To Opening Stock	17,500	By Sales	2,65,000
To Purchases	1,12,600	By Goods withdrawn	
To Productive Wages	7,000	by Neela	800
To Works Manager"s Salary	5,600	By Closing Stock	19,000
To Gross Profit	1,42,100		
	2,84,800		**2,84,800**

Profit & Loss Account for the year ended 31st March 2007

Particulars	Rs.	Particulars	Rs.
To Salaries & Wages	4,600	By Gross Profit	1,42,100
To Office Expenses	4,300	By Commission	2,500
To Legal Expenses	3,300	By Interest	1,600
To Bad Debts	1,900		
To Commission	1,800		
To Depreciation			
Loose Tools	4,200		
Land & Building	12,500		
To Net Profit			
Neela 56,800			
Sheela 56,800	113600		
	1,46,200		**1,46,200**

Balance Sheet as on 31st March 2007

Liabilities	Rs.	Rs.	Assets	Rs.	Rs.
Capital	1,10,000		Cash in hand		6,000
Accounts Neela	56,800		Bills		4,000
: balance (+)	20,000		Receivable		42,000
Net Profit	800	1,46,000	Investments		67,500
(–) Drawings	1,05,000		Sundry		19,000
(–) Goods taken	56,800		Debtors Stock	28,000	38,000
	30,000		Patents		
Sheela : balance		1,31,800	Loose Tools		23,800
(+) Net Profit			(–) Dep^n	1,25,000	65,000
(–) Drawings		88,000	15%	12,500	80,000
		92,000	Furniture		1,12,500
Bank Overdraft			Goodwill		
Sundry Creditors			Land & Building		
		4,57,800			4,57,800

Illustration 2 : From the following Trial balance of Ram and Shyam. You are required to prepare Trading and Profit & Loss Account for the year ending 31st Dec. 2006 and balance sheet as on that date after consideration the adjustments given below.

Trial Balance as on 31st March, 2006

Dr.   Cr.

Particulars	Rs.	Particulars	Rs.
Stock (01.04.05)	35,000	Sales	3,30,000
Salary and Wages	9,200	Discount	4,800
Cash	10,000	Creditors	20,000
Purchases	2,25,200	Bank Overdraft	10,000
Sundry Expenses	8,600	Interest on Investments	7,200
Productive Wages	14,000	Capital Accounts	
Bills Receivable	8,000	Ram	60,000
Law charges	3,000	Shyam	40,000
Bad Debts	1,000		
Works Expenses	6,000		
Commission	3,000		
Investments	20,000		
Debtors	40,000		
Trade Marks	8,000		
Tools and Equipments	6,000		

Goodwill	13,000		
Building	50,000		
	4,72,000		**4,72,000**

Adjustments :

1) Partners shares Profit and Losses in the equal ratio.

2) Closing Stock cost price Rs.40,000/- market value Rs.45,000/-.

3) Uninsured goods worth Rs.10,000/- were lost by fire.

4) Unpaid Salary and Wages Rs.2,100/-.

Trading Account for the year ended 31st December 2006

Particulars	Rs.	Particulars	Rs.
To Opening Stock	35,000	By Sales	3,30,000
To Purchases	2,25,200	By Uninsured Goods	
To Productive Wages	14,000	lost by fire	10,000
To Works Expenses	6,000	By Closing Stock	40,000
To Gross Profit c/d	99,800		
	3,80,000		**3,80,000**

Profit & Loss Account for the year ended 31st December 2006

Particulars		Rs.	Particulars	Rs.
To Sundry Expnses		8,600	By Gross Profit	99,800
To Law Charg;		3,000	By Discount	4,800
To Bad Debts		1,000	By Interest on	
To Commission		3,000	Investment	7,200
To Salaries	9,200			
(+) Outstanding	2,100	11,300		
To Uninsured Goods				
lost by fire		10,000		
To Net Profit				
Ram	37,450			
Shyam	37,450	74,900		
		1,11,800		**1,11,800**

110

Balance Sheet as on 31st December 2006

Liabilities	Rs.	Rs.	Assets	Rs.	Rs.
Capital			Cash		10,000
Accounts Ram	60,000		Bills		8,000
: balance (+)	37,450	97,450	Receivable		20,000
Net Profit			Investments		40,000
	40,000		Debtors		8,000
	37,450	77,450	Trade marks		
Shyam :					6,000
balance			Tools and		40,000
(+) Net Profit		20,000	Equipments		12,000
		10,000	Closing		13,000
Creditors			Stock		50,000
Bank Overdraft		2,100	Furniture		
Outstanding			Goodwill		
		2,07,000			**2,07,000**

Illustration 3 : (Goods withdrawn, Loss by Fire)

From the following Trial Balance of Jagan and Magan, you are required to prepare a Trading and Profit and Loss Account for the year ended 31st March 2010 and the Balance Sheet as on that date, after taking into the consideration the additional information :

Trial Balance as on 31st March 2010

Particulars	Debit (Rs.)	Credit (Rs.)
Opening Stock	17,500	-
Salaries and Wages	4,600	-
Cash in hand	5,000	-
Purchases and Sales	1,12,600	1,65,000
Office Expenses	4,300	-
Productive Wages	7,000	-
Bills Receivable	4,000	-
Legal Expenses	1,500	-
Bad Debts	500	-
Works Manager"s Salary	3,000	-
Commission	1,500	2,400
Investments	10,000	-
Debtors and Creditors	20,000	10,000

Patents	4,000	-
Loose Tools	3,000	-
Furniture	6,000	-
Goodwill	6,500	-
Interest on Investment	-	3,600
Land and Building	25,000	-
Capital Accounts :		
Jagan	-	30,000
Magan	-	20,000
	2,36,000	**2,36,000**

Adjustments :

1. Partners share Profits and Losses in their capital ratio.
2. The Closing Stock – Cost Rs.20,000/- Market Value Rs.22,500/-
3. Jagan has withdrawn goods worth Rs.600/- for his personal use.
4. Uninsured goods worth Rs.5,000/- were destroyed by fire.
5. Rs.225/- written off as bad debts from Debtors.
6. Outstanding Salaries and Wages Rs.400/-.
7. Depreciation on Land and Building at 7½ %.

Solution :

M/s. Jagan and Magan
Trading, Profit & Loss Account for the year ended 31-03-2005

Dr.   Cr.

Particulars	Rs.	Particulars	Rs.
To Opening Stock	17,500	By Sales	1,65,000
To Purchases	1,12,600	By Goods withdrawn	600
To Productive Wages	7,000	(Jagan) By Goods Lost by	5,000
To Work Manager"s	3,000	Fire	20,000
Salary	50,500	By Closing Stock	
To Gross Profit c/d			
	1,90,600		**1,90,600**
To Salaries &s Wage 4,600	5,000	By Gross Profit c/d	50,500
(+)	4,300	By Commission	2,400
Outstanding	1,500	By Interest on Investment	3,600
To Office 500			
Expense To —225	725		
Legal Expense	1,500		
To Bad Debts	5,000		
(+) Additional			
B.D. To pital A/c	1,875		

112

Jagan (3/5)	21,960				
Magan (2/5)	14,640	36,600			
		56,500			56,500

Balance Sheet as on 31-3-2005

Liabilities	Rs.	Rs.	Assets	Rs.	Rs.
Jagan"s Capital			Goodwill		6,500
Balance b/d	30,000		Land &	25,000	
(+) Net Profit	21,960		Building (-)	1,875	23,125
	51,960		Depreciation		6,000
(-) Drawings	600	51,360	Furniture		3,000
Magan"s			Loose		4,000
Capital	20,000		Tools		10,000
Balance b/d	14,640	34,640	Patents	20,000	4,000
(+) Net Profit		10,000	Investment	225	
Creditors		5,000	s		19,775
Bank Overdraft		400	Bills Receivable		20,000
					5,000
		1,01,40			1,01,40

7.12 EXERCISES

7.12.1 Theory Questions :

a) What is Partnership Deed?

b) What are provisions of Partnership Act relating Accounts of Partnership?

c) State different methods of maintaining Capital Account.

d) What are provisions of Indian Partnership Act 1932 in respect of interest on Capital, Drawings and Loan"s from Partner?

e) What are different types of Partners?

7.12.2 Practical Questions

Q.1 R and K are partners in a firm sharing Profits and Losses in the ratio 3:2. Their trial balance on 31/03/2010 was as follows:

Trial Balance as on 31st March, 2010

Particulars	Debit (Rs.)	Particulars	Credit (Rs.)
Opening Stock	26,700	R"s Capital	36,000
Purchases	60,000	K"s Capital	24,000
Plant & Machinery	21,000	Sales	1,50,000
Furniture	1,400	Creditors	4,400
Carriage	1,500	Unpaid Wages	900
Wages and Salaries	45,000	Return Outwards	1,500
Traveling Expenses	9,750		
Taxes and Rent	1,950		
Bills Receivable	3,000		
Debtors	24,000		
Return Inwards	3,750		
Bank	13,500		
Commission	1,500		
Bad Debts	600		
Cash in hand	150		
R"s Drawing	1,800		
K"s Drawing	1,200		
	2,16,800		2,16,800

Prepare Trading and Profit & Loss Account for the year ending 31/03/2010 and the Balance Sheet as on that date after making the following adjustments.

1) Closing Stock was valued at Rs.27,900/-.

2) Depreciation Plant & Machinery by 10% p.a.

Q.2 Usha, Uma and Urmila were partners sharing profits & losses in the ratio 2:2:1 respectively. The trial balance of their firm on 31st March, 2010 was follows :

Trial balance

Particulars	Debit (Rs.)	Particulars	Credit (Rs.)
Opening Stock	8,000	**Capital Accounts :**	
Purchases	50,000	Usha	20,000
Wages	7,000	Uma	20,000
Carriage Inwards	2,000	Urmil	10,000
Electricity &	1,900	a	
Insurance Return	4,000	**Current Accounts :**	4,000
Inwards Salaries	9,700	Usha	2,550
Bad debts	4,100	Uma	500
Bills Receivable	7,800	Urmil	90,000
Debtors	10,200	a Sales	4,400
Building	30,000	Rent received	30,000
Traveling Expenses	4,900	Creditors	350
Cash at Bank	5,900	Sundry income	
Prepaid Insurance	100		
Vehicle	10,000		
Audit Fees	700		
	1,18,800		**1,81,800**

Prepare Trading and Profit & Loss Account for the year ended 31st March, 2010 and the Balance Sheet as on that date after making the following adjustments :

1) Goods worth Rs.6,000/- were destroyed by fire and Insurance Company admitted the claim for Rs.5,300/-.

2) Outstanding Expenses were Wages of Rs.1,500/- and Electricity Rs.400/-.

3) Closing Stock was valued at Rs.42,500/-.

4) Provide Salary to Partner Usha Rs.1,000/- p.a. and Interest on Capital @ 12% p.a.

Q.3 From the following trial balance prepare the Trading and Profit & Loss Account for the year ending 31st March, 2010 and a balance sheet as on that date, after taking into considerations the following adjustments.

Trial Balance as on 31st March, 2010

Particulars	Debit (Rs.)	Particulars	Credit (Rs.)
Opening Stock	20,000	Bills Payable	10,000
Sundry Debtors	28,000	Returns Outwards	2,500
Purchases	40,000	Sundry Creditors	21,500
Wages	8,500	Sales	70,000
Salaries	2,700	10% Loan (taken on 1st Oct. 2009)	3,000
Office Expenses	2,445		
Insurance	1,300	Commission	1,400
Plant & Machinery	30,000	Discount Received	500
Rent	1,800	Rent Received	700
Traveling Expenses	1,400	**Capital of Partners :**	
Return Inwards	3,500	A	40,000
Land & Building	44,800	B	50,000
Bills Receivable	4,000		
Bank Balance	6,655		
Furniture	2,400		
Sundry Expenses	1,400		
Advertisement	700		
	1,99,600		**1,99,600**

Adjustments :

1) Stock as on 31.03.2010 was valued at Rs.25,000/-.

2) Outstanding Salaries Rs.6,000/- not provided.

3) Prepaid Insurance Rs.250/-.

4) Provide Interest on Capital @ 10% p.a.

☐☐☐☐☐

Unit - 8
COST ACCOUNTING

Unit Structure:

8.0 OBJECTIVES

After studying this chapter, you should be able to understand:

- Need for Cost Accounting

- Meaning of Cost, Costing and Cost Accounting

- Objectives of Cost Accounting

- Classification of Cost

- Elements of Cash

- Methods of Costing

8.1 INTRODUCTION

Cost Accounting is the system of accounting which is concerned with determination of costs of doing something which can be manufacturing or rendering service or even conducting any activity or function. The objective of Cost Accounting is to render detailed and useful information for guidance to Management.

Financial accounting is developed over the time to record, summarise and present the financial transaction or events which can be expressed in terms of money. This function was primarily concerned with record keeping, leading to preparation of Profit and Loss Account and Balance Sheet. The information obtained through financial statements is useful to the Management or Owner in several respects.

However, the information provided by financial accounting is not sufficient for several purposes of decision making in many areas such as : determining output level, determining product selection – addition or dropping or changing product combination in the case of multi product company, determining or revising prices of products, whether Profit earned is optimum as compared with competitors and in comparison to earlier years.

The need of data for such details lead to the development of Cost Accountancy.

8.2 LIMITATIONS OF FINANCIAL ACCOUNTING

Financial accounting does not help in day to day management of the organisation. Cost Accounting has emerged mainly because of certain limitations of financial accounting, which are summarized as follows –

1) Financial accounting provides information about the business as a whole. But it does not reveal Profit or loss of each department or product or process.

2) Material and supplies can not be controlled effectively. There is no proper system of control of material which may in losses in the form of deterioration, scrap, misappropriation etc.

3) It does not provide cost information for fixation of prices of products and services.

4) It does not classify the expenses into direct and indirect, fixed and variable and controllable and non-controllable.

5) There is no system of recording loss of labour, i.e. idle time and labour cost is not recorded by jobs, processes etc.

6) Financial accounting is a historical record. It does not help in controlling the cost.

7) It does not facilitate cost reduction which is very important and necessary for cost control.

8) It fails to supply useful information to management for taking various decisions like replacement of labour by machine, introduction of new product, make or buy, selection of most profitable product mix etc.

Therefore, Cost Accounting has developed as a separate branch of accounting. Both cost and financial accounting are concerned with systematic recording and presentation of financial data.

Financial accounting reveals Profit / Loss of business as a whole for a certain period. But Cost Accounting reveals Profit / Loss of different product lines. It helps to decide profitability of each process or each product.

8.3   MEANING OF COST, COSTING and COST ACCOUNTING

8.3.1 Cost :

Institute of Cost and Works Accountants of India, defines cost as "measurement, in monetary terms, of the amount of resources used for the purpose of production of goods or rendering services".

Thus the term cost means the amount of expenditure, actual or notional incurred or attributable to a given thing. It can be regarded as the price paid for attaining the objective. For e.g. Material cost is the price of materials acquired for manufacturing a product.

8.3.2 Costing :

The term costing has been defined as "the techniques and processes of ascertainment of costs. Weldon, has defined costing as, "the classifying recording   and   appropriateallocation of   expenditure for the determination of costs the relation of these costs to sale value and the ascertainment of profitability." Threfore costing involves the following steps.

1) Ascertaining and Collecting of Costs

2) Analysis or Classification of Costs

3) Allocating total costs to a particular thing i.e. product, a contract or a process.

Thus costing simply means cost finding by any process or technique.

8.3.3 Cost Accounting :

Cost Accounting is a formal system of accounting by means of which cost of products or service, are ascertained and controlled.

"Weldon"   defines   Cost   Accounting   as   "Classifying, recording   and   appropriate allocation   of   expenditure   for determination of costs of products or services and   for   the presentation of suitably arranged data for the purpose of control and guidance of management."

Therefore, Cost Accounting is the application of costing principles, methods and techniques in the ascertainment of costs and analysis of savings or / and excesses as compared with previous experience or with standards.   It provides, detailed cost information to   various levels of   management   for   efficient performance of their functions.   The information supplied by Cost Accounting as a tool of management for making optimum use of scarce resources and ultimately add to the profitability of business.

> Cost Accounting = Costing (+) Application of Cost control methods and ascertainment of profitability (+) Presentation of relevant information for managerial decision making.

8.4 COST CENTRE AND COST UNITS

8.4.1 Cost Centre :

It is a location, person or item of equipment for which cost may be ascertained and used for the purpose of cost control. It is a convenient unit of the organisation for which cost may be ascertained. The main purpose of ascertainment of cost is to control the cost and fill up the responsibility of the person who is incharge of the cost centre.

- **Types of cost centers : I.**

Personal Cost Centre :

It consists of a person or group of persons. e.g.
machine operator, salesmen, etc.

II. Impersonal Cost Centre :

It consists of a location or an item of equipment or group of these. E.g. Factory, Machine etc.

III. Operational Cost Centre :

This consists of machines or persons carrying on similar operations.

IV. Process Cost Centre :

This consists of a continuous sequence of operation or specific operations.

V. Production Cost Centre :

This is the centre where actual production takes place or these include, those departments that are directly engaged in manufacturing activity and contribute to the content and form of finished product. e.g. Cutting, Assembly and Finishing Departments etc.

VI. Service Cost Centre :

This is the Centre which renders services to production centres. These contribute to the production process in an indirect manner. e.g. Stores department, Repairs and Maintainance department, H.R. Department, Purchase Department etc.

8.4.2 Cost unit :

It is a unit of product, service or time in terms of which cost are ascertained or expressed. It is basically, a unit of quantity of product or service in relation to which costs may be ascertained or expressed.

Few examples of cost unit are given below.

Name of Industry	Cost unit
Textiles	Meter, yards
Transport	Passenger km
Power Paints	Kilowatt – hour
Iron and Steel	Litre & Tonne
Canteen Chemical	Per meal & Litre, kilogram
Readymade Garments	Number
Ptrol	Litre

8.5 OBJECTIVES OF COST ACCOUNTING

Objectives of Cost Accounting are as follows :

1) **Ascertain Cost :** To ascertain the cost of product or a services reveled and enable measurement of profit by proper valuation of inventory.

2) **Analyse Costs :** To analysis costs or to classify the expenses under different heads of accounts viz. material, labour, expenses etc.

3) **Allocate and Apportion the Costs :** To allocate or charge the direct expenses or specific costs such as Raw Material, Labour to particular product, contract or process and to distribute common expenses to each product, contract or process on a suitable basis.

4) **Cost Reporting :** Cost Reporting or presentation includes :

   a) What to report i.e. what is the nature of information to be presented?

   b) Whom to Report i.e. to whom the report is to be addressed.

   c) When to Report i.e. when the report is to be presented i.e. Daily weekly monthly yearly etc.

   d) How to Report i.e. in what format the report is to be presented.

5) **Assist the Management :** Cost Accounting assist the management in the following ways

   a) Indicate to the management any inefficiencies and extent of various forms of waste of Raw Material, Time, Expenses etc.

   b) Help the management in fixing of selling price.

   c) Provide information to enable management to take decision of various types.

6) **Cost Control :** Cost Accounting assist the management in cost control. Cost control includes the following stages.

   a) Setting up of targets of cast and production for each period.

b) Measuring the actual figures of performance relating to cost, production etc. for the period concerned.

c) The figures of actual performance are to be compared with the targets to find out the variation.

d) Analysing the variance, whether favourable or adverse.

e) Immediate action has to be taken in case of adverse variation.

7) **Controlling Inventory :** Assist the management in controlling Inventory of Raw Material, goods in process, finished goods, spares and consumables etc.

8) **Optimum Product Mix :** Advise the management in deciding optimum product mix merits and demerits of alterative courses of action viz. make of buy decisions, introduction or Automation mechanization, rationalization, system of production etc.

9) **Future Policies :** Advise management on future policies regarding Expansion, growth, capital investment, etc.

8.6   CLASSIFICATION OF COST

Classification is the process of grouping costs according to their common characteristics. It is a systematic placement of like items together according to their common features. There are various ways of classifying costs, according to their common features as given below.

Chart showing classification of cost :

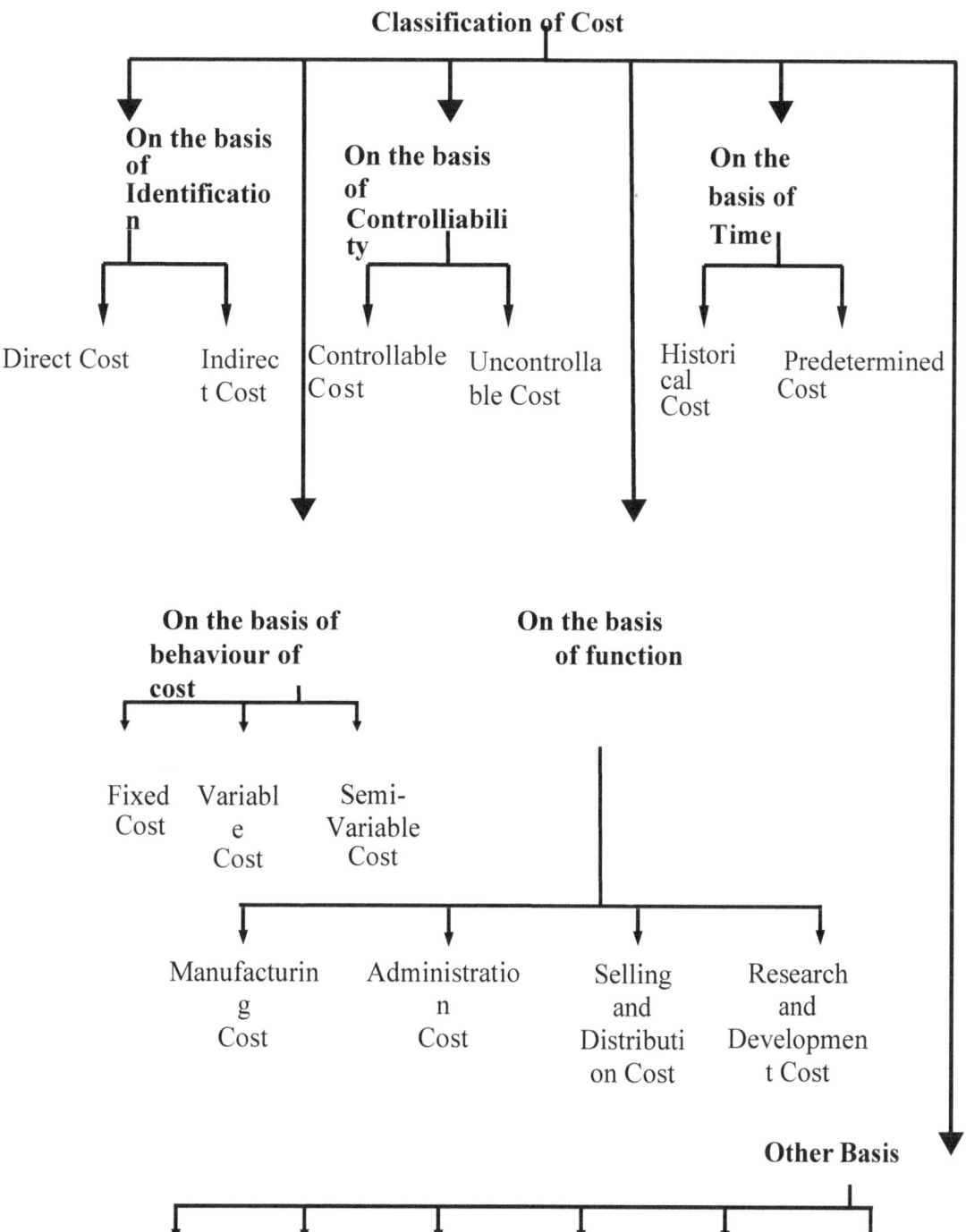

I   On the basis of Identification :

On the basis of identification of cost with cost units or jobs or processes, costs are classified into –

1) Direct Costs

2) Indirect Costs

1) **Direct Costs :** These are the costs which are incurred for and conveniently identified with a particular cost unit process or department.   These are the expenditures which can be directly allocated to a particular job, product or an activity. Eg. Cost of Raw Material used, wages paid to labourers etc.

2) **Indirect Costs :** These are general costs and are incurred for the benefit of a number of cost units, processes or departments. These costs can not be conveniently identified with a particular cost unit or cost centre.
Example : Depreciation of Machinery, Insurance, Lighting, Power, Rent of Building, Managerial Salaries, etc.

II   On the basis of behaviour of Cost

Behaviour means change in cost due to change in output. Costs behave differently when the level of production rises or falls. Certain costs change in direct proportion with production level while other costs remain unchanged. As such on the basis of behaviour of cost – costs are classified into

1) Fixed Costs.

2) Variable Costs.

3) Semi Variable Costs.

1) **Fixed Costs :** It is that portion of the total cost which remain constant irrespective of output upto the capacity limit. It is the cost which does not very with the change in the volume of activity in the short run. These costs are not affected by temporary fluctuation in the activity of an enterprise. These are also known as period costs as it is concerned with period. Rent of premises, tax and insurance, staff salaries, are the examples of fixed cost.
Characteristics of Fixed Cost are :

1) Large in value

2) Fixed amount within an output range

3) Fixed cost per unit decreases with increased output

4) Indirect Cost

5) Lesser degree of controllability

6) Influence Variable Cost and Working Capital

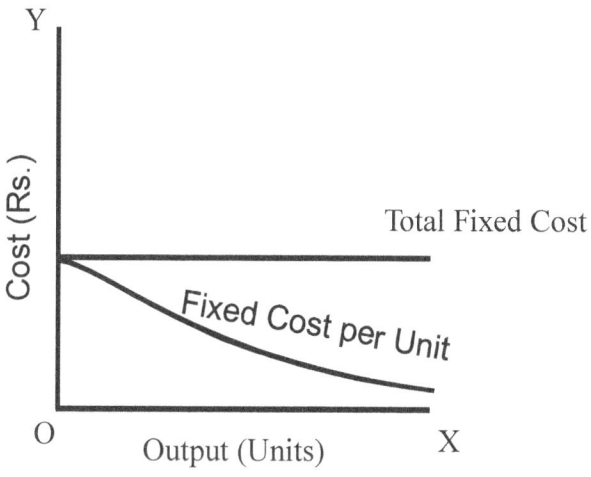

Behaviour of Fixed Cost

2) **Variable Cost:** It is that cost which directly very with the volume of activity. In other words, it is a cost which changes according to the changes in the volume of output. It tends to very in direct proportion to output.It means when the volume of output increases, total variable cost also increases when the volume of output decreases, total variable cost also decreases. But the variable cost per unit remains same. Direct material, Direct Labour, Direct Expenses are the examples of variable costs. Characteristics of Variable Cost are :

1) Total cost changes in direct proportion to the change in total output.

2) Cost per unit remains content.

3) It is quite divisible.

4) It is identifiable with the individual cost unit.

5) Such costs are controlled by functional manager.

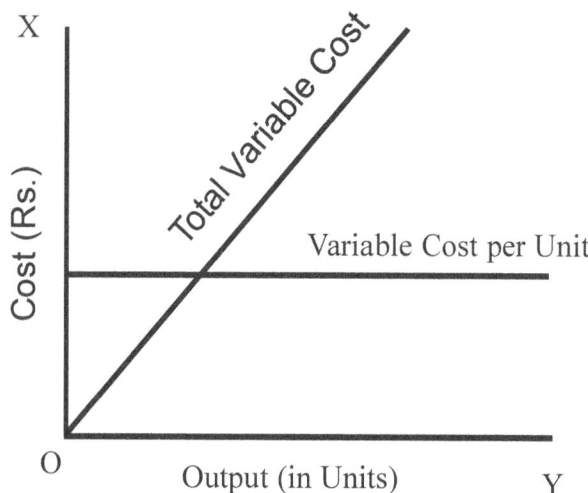

Behaviour of Variable Cost

125

3) Semi-Variable Cost : This is also referred as semi-fixed costs.
These costs include both a fixed and a variable component. i.e. These are partly fixed and partly variable. They remain constant upto a certain level and registers change afterwards. These costs vary in some degree with volume but not in direct or same proportion. Such costs are fixed only in relation to specified constant condition.

For example : Repairs and maintainance of machinery, telephone charges, maintainance of building, supervision, professional tax, compensation for accidents, light and power etc.

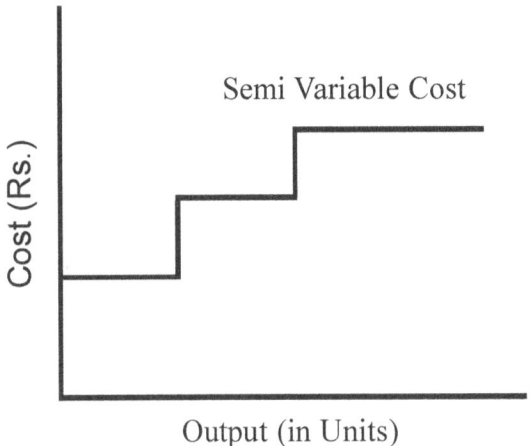

Behaviour of Semi-Variable Cost

III. On the basis of Controllability

On the basis of controllability, costs are classified into two types :

1) Controllable Cost

2) Uncontrollable Cost

1) **Controllable Cost :** These are the costs which can not be influenced or controlled by the concerned cost centre or responsibility centre. These given level of management authority.

126

2) **Uncontrollable Cost :** These are the costs, which can not be influenced or controlled by the action of a specific member of an enterprise. For eg. it is very difficult to control costs like factory rent, managerial salaries etc.

The important points to be noted regarding this classification. First, controllable cost can not be distinguished from non- controllable costs, without specifying the level and scope of management authority. It means cost which is uncontrollable at one level of management may be controllable at another level of management. Eg. Rent and Factory Building may be beyond control for the production department but can be controlled by the administrative department by negotiations. Secondly all costs are controllable in the long run and at the some appropriate management level.

IV   On the basis of Functions

An organisation performs many functions. On the basis of functions costs can be classified as follows :

1) **Manufacturing Costs :** It is the cost of all items involved in the manufacturing of a product or service. It includes all direct costs and all indirect costs related to the production. It includes cost of direct materials, direct labour, direct expenses, and overhead expenses related to production. Overhead expenses, means all indirect costs involved in the production process. This is termed as factory overhead or manufacturing overheads. Eg.Salaries of staff for production department, technical supervision, Expenses of stores department, Depreciation of Plant and Machinery, Repairs and maintenance of Factory Building and Machineries etc.

2) **Administration Cost :** These are costs incurred for general management of an organisation. It is the cost which is incurred for formulating the policy, directing the organisation of controlling the operations. These are in the nature of indirect costs and are also termed as administrative overhead. Eg. Salaries of Administrative Stall, General Office expenses like rent, lighting, telephone, stationery, postage etc.

3) **Selling and Distribution Costs :** Selling costs are the indirect costs relating to selling of products or services. They include all indirect cost in sales management for the organisation. Selling costs include all expenses relating to regular sales and sales promotion activities. Examples of expenses which are included in selling costs are :

1) Salaries, Commission and traveling expenses for sales personnel

2) Advertisement cost

3) Legal Expenses for debt realization

4) Market research cost

5) Show room expenses

6) Discount allowed

7) Sample and free gifts

8) Rent on Sales room

9) After sale services

Distribution costs are the costs incurred in handling a product from the time it is completed in the works until it reaches the ultimate consumer. Distribution expenses include all these expenses which are incurred in connection with making the goods available to customers. These expenses include the following.

1) Packing charges

2) Loading charges

3) Carriage on Sales

4) Rent of warehouse

5) Insurance and lighting of warehouse

6) Transportation costs

7) Salaries of godown keeper, driver, packing staff etc.

4) **Research and Development Cost :** Research and development costs are incurred to discover new ideas, processes, products by experiment. It includes the cost of the process which begins with the implementation of the decision to produce or improved product.

V   On the basis of Time

On the basis of time of computation, costs are classified into historical costs and predetermined costs.

1) **Historical Costs :** These are the costs which are ascertained after these have been incurred. Historical costs are then nothing but actual costs. They represent the costs of actual operational performance. These costs are not available until after the completion of manufacturing operations.

2) **Pre determined Costs :** These are the future costs which are ascertained in advance of production on the basis of a specification of all the factors affecting cost and cost data. Predetermined costs are future costs determined in advance on the basis of standards or estimates. These costs are extensively used for the purpose of planning and control.

VI   Other Basis

1) **Normal Cost :** Normal cost may be defined as a cost which is normally incurred on expected lines at a given level of output, in the condition in which that level of output in normally attained. This cost is a part of production.

2) **Abnormal Cost :** Abnormal cost is that cost which is not normally incurred at a given level of output, in the condition in which that level of output is normally attained. Such cost is over and above the normal cost and is not treated as a part of the cost of production.

3) **Avoidable Cost :** The cost which can be avoided under the present conditions is an avoidable cost. These are the costs which under given conditions of performance efficiency should not have been incurred. They are logically associated with some activity and situation and are ascertained by the difference of actual cost with the happening of the situation and the normal cost. Eg. when spoilage occurs in manufacturing in excess of normal limit, the resulting cost of spoilage is avoidable cost.

4) **Unavoidable Cost :** The cost which can not be avoidable under the present condition is an unavoidable cost. They are inescapable costs which are essentially to be incurred within the limits or norms provided for. It is the cost that must be incurred under a programme of business restriction.

CHECK YOUR PROGRESS
- Draw the chart showing Classification of Cost.
- Define the following terms:
    1. Costing
    2. Cost Accounting
    3. Impersonal cost center

4. Service Cost center
5. Direct Cost
6. Uncontrollable cost
7. Predetermined cost

- Give Examples:
    1. Fixed cost
    2. Variable cost
    3. Semi variable cost
    4. Manufacturing cost
    5. Administration cost
    6. Selling cost
    7. Distribution Cost

8.7   ELEMENTS OF COST

A cost is composed of three elements i.e. material, labour and expenses. Each of these elements may be direct or indirect. This is shown as follows :

Direct Costs	**Indirect Costs**
Direct Material	Indirect Material
Direct Labour	Indirect Labour
Direct Expenses	Indirect Expenses

8.7.1 Material Cost

It is the cost of material of any nature used for the purpose of production of a product or a service.   Materials may be Direct Material or Indirect Material.

- **Direct material :** It is the cost of basic raw material used for manufacturing a product. Direct materials generally became a part of the finished product. No finished product can be manufactured without basic raw material. This cost is easily identifiable and chargeable to the product. For e.g. Leather in leather products, Steel in steel furniture, Cotton in textile etc. Direct material includes the following.

1) All materials specially purchased for production or the process.

2) All components purchased for production or the process.

3) Material transferred from one cost centre to another or one process to another process.

4) Primary packaging materials, wrappings, cardboard boxes etc necessary for production or protection of product.

However, in many cases, though a material forms a part of the finished product, yet it is not treated as direct material. Eg. nails used in furniture, thread used in stitching garments etc. This is because value of such materials is so small that it is quite difficult to measure it.

- **Indirect material :** It is the cost of material other than direct material which cannot be charged to the product directly. It can not be treated as part of the product. These are minor in importance. It is also known as expenses materials. It is the material which cannot be allocated to the product but can be apportioned to the cost units.

Examples : Lubricants, Cotton waste, Grease, Oil, Small tools, Minor items like thread in dress making, nails in furniture (nuts, bolts in furniture) etc.

Therefore, indirect materials can not be easily identified with specific job. They may not vary directly with the output. It is considered as a part of overheads.

8.7.2 Labour Cost

This is the cost of remuneration in the form of wages, Salaries, Commissions, Bonuses etc. paid to the workers and employees of an organisation.

- **Direct Labour Cost :** Direct Labour Cost is the amount of wages paid to those workers who are engaged on the manufacturing line. It consists of wages paid to workers engaged in converting of raw materials into finished products. The amount of wages can be conveniently identified with a particular line, product, job or process. These workers directly handle machines on the production line. Direct wages include payment made to the following group of workers.

1) Labour engaged on the actual production of the product

2) Labour engaged in aiding the operation viz. supervisor, foremen, shop Clerks and worker on internal transport.

3) Inspectors, Analysts, needed for such production.

Example : Carpenter in furniture making unit, tailor in readymade wear unit, Labour in construction work etc.

- **Indirect Labour Cost :** It is the amount of wages paid to those workers who are not engaged on the manufacturing line. It is of general character and can not be directly identified with a particular cost unit. This indirect labour is not directly engaged in the production operations but such labour assist or help in production operations. It can not be easily identified with specific job, contract of work order. It may not vary directly with the output. It is treated as part of overheads.

Example : Labour in Human Resource department, Labour in payroll department, Labour in stores, Labour in Securities Department, Labour in power house department etc.

8.7.3 Expenses

All costs other than material and labour are termed as expenses. It is defined as the cost of services provided to an undertaking and the notional cost of the use of owned assets.

- **Direct Expenses :** It is the amount of expenses which is directly chargeable to product manufactured or which may be allocated to product directly. It can be easily identified with the product. These are the expenses which are specifically incurred in connection with a particular job or cost unit. They are also called as chargeable expenses.

Example : Hire of special plant for a particular job, Travelling expenses in securing a particular contract, Carriage paid for materials purchased for specific job, Royalty paid in mining or production etc.

- **Indirect Expenses :** All indirect costs other than indirect materials and indirect labour costs, are termed as indirect expenses. It is the amount of expenses which can not be charged to the product directly. These can not be directly identified with particular job, process or work order and are common to cost units" or cost centres. Indirect expenses include factory expenses, administrative overheads, selling and distribution expenses etc.

8.7.4 Overhead

This is the aggregate of indirect material cost, indirect labour cost and Indirect expenses.

Thus overhead= Indirect Material + Indirect Labour + Indirect Expenses

8.8 METHODS OF COSTING

Methods of Cost Accounting signify the systems used to assign cost elements to cost objects. These are the procedures by which product costs are accumulated. Different methods of cost determination are used because business vary in their nature and the type of products or services they produce. Following are the different methods of costing.

8.8.1 Job costing and Batch Costing:

Job costing is designed to accumulate cost data for a manufacturing firm which produces goods to specific order. It is also known as specific orders costing or production order costing. According to "ICMA", London, it is that category of basic costing method which is applicable where the work consists of separate contract job or batches each of which is authorized by specific order or contract. It is followed by manufacturing and non- manufacturing concerns. It is employed in industries in which –

a) A production is done on the basis of customer"s own specifications.

b) Products are manufactured in distinguishable lots.

c) Products are not uniform.

d) It is practical to maintain a separate record of each lot from the time production is begun until it is completed.

Following is the list of concerns which generally employ job costing method.

a) Printing Work.

b) Design Engineering Concerns.

c) Repair Works.

d) Construction companies.

e) Furniture makers.

f) Hardware industry.

g) Automobile garages.

h) Interior decoration etc.

Batch Costing

It is a form of job costing in which a batches of identical products is taken as the cost unit. It is used when production consists of limited repetition work and a definite number of articles are manufactured in each batch to be held in stock for sale to customers generally. Thus batch is a cost unit consisting of a group of identical units.

Batch costing is applied in the manufacture of shoes, readymade garments, component parts of cars, radios, watches etc and manufacture of drugs, engineering equipments etc.

For eg. in foot wear industry it is not just economical to manufacture a pair of shoes to meet the requirement of one customer. But batches say 500 to 5000 shoes of each size, style colour etc are economically made and held in stock for sale on demand.

8.8.2 Contract Costing:

It is a method of costing in which each contract is taken as a separate costing unit for the purpose of cost ascertainment and control. The objective is find out the Profit or loss on each contract separately. Contract costing is employed in business undertakings engaged in building construction, road construction, bridge construction, dam construction and other civil engineering works, ship building etc.

Contracts are generally of large size. A contract generally takes more than one year to complete. Work on contract is carried out at the site of the contracts and not in factory premises. Payments by the customer (contractee) are made at various stages of completion of the contract based on architects certificate for the completed stage.

8.8.3 Process Costing:

It is a method of costing used to ascertain the cost of the product at each process operation or stage of manufacture where processes are carried on. According to ICMA London, "It is that form of operation costing where standardized goods are produced."

Process costing is used to ascertain the cost of product at each stage of manufacture where material is passed through various operations to obtain a final product. This method of costing is used by those concern which manufacture articles of uniform standards. These concerns manufacture articles on a continuous flow basis.

Each process is treated as a cost centre and separate account is opened for each process. All costs related to a process are debited to its process account. The output passing through the process is also recorded. The output of one process becomes the input of next process and so on until the finished product is obtained. This method is suitable for Textile mills, Chemical works, Oil refining, Cement manufactures, Paper Manufacture, Steel production, Paint manufacture, Sugar works, Plastic manufactures etc.

8.8.4 Single (output) or unit costing:

It is a method of costing in which cost is ascertained in convenient units of product turned out by continuous manufacturing activity. The unit of costing is chosen according to the nature of product. This method of costing is used in those industries, in which the production consists of a single product or a few varieties of the same product with variations in size, shape, quality etc. and production is uniform and on continuous basis.

Examples of industries in which this method is commonly used are : Cement, Steel, Sugar, Paper brick works, dairies etc. Cost of units in these industries are a tonne of cement, or steel, or sugar, 1000 bricks, a gallon of milk etc.

This method is also known as single costing.

8.8.5 Operating Costing:

It is a method of costing which is used in those industries, which are engaged in providing services such as transport, electricity etc. The cost of providing a service is termed as operating cost. Operating costing is used in those industries, where services rendered to customers are of unique and standardized type.

The selection of a suitable cost unit (unit of service) is very important. The cost unit may be different for different type of industries. A few examples are given below.

Undertakings	**Cost Unit**
Transport	Per passenger km
Hospital	Per bed per day
Hotel	Per room per day
Electricity	Per kilowatt hour
Cinema	Per seat per show

8.8.5 Operation Costing:

Under this method each operation is treated as a cost centre. Costs are accumulated in each operation instead of each process. This method is used by industries engaged in repetitive mass production with continuous flow of work. These industries could be those engaged in the manufacture of leather products, toys, bicycles, ceiling fans, weighing machines etc.

8.9 KEY POINTS

- **Cost :** It is the amount of expenditure, actual or notional incurred on a given thing.

- **Costing :** It is process of ascertaining the cost.

- **Cost Centre :** It is a convenient unit for which cost may be ascertained.

- **Cost Unit :** It is a unit of product or service for which cost is ascertained.

- **Cost Control :** It involves comparing actual cost with the target and taking remedial action.

Objectives of –

- **Cost Accounting :** Ascertain Cost, Analyse Cost, allocate and apportion Cost, Cost Reporting, Assist the management, Cost control, Optimum product mix, Future policies.

- **Elements of Cost :** Direct Cost – Direct material, Direct labour, Direct expenses. Indirect Cost – Indirect material, Indirect labour, Indirect expenses.

- **Methods of Costing :** Job and Batch Costing, Contract Costing, Process Costing, Output Costing Operating Costing, Operation Costing.

8.10 ADDITIONAL READINGS

1) Cost Accounting – Principles and practice by M.N. Arora

2) Cost Accounting – An introduction by Nigam and Jain

3) Cost Accounting – Chopade and Choudhary

8.11 EXERCISE

1) What is meant by Cost Accounting? Explain in brief different ways of Cost Classification.

2) What is Cost Accounting? What are the elements of Cost Accounting?

3) What is Cost Accounting? Explain the methods of Costing.

4) What is Cost Accounting and what are the objectives of Cost Accounting?

□□□□□

Unit - 9
FINANCIAL MANAGEMENT

Unit Structure:

9.0   Objectives

9.1   Meaning

9.2   Scope of Financial Management

9.3   Role of Financial Management

9.4   Functional areas of Financial Management

9.5   Various Financial Management Tools

9.6   Exercise

9.0   OBJECTIVES

After studying the unit the students will be able to:

- Know the meaning of Financial Management.

- Explain the Scope and role of Financial Management.

- Elaborate the Functional areas of Financial Management.

- Understand the various tools of FM, advantages and disadvantages of various tools.

9.1   MEANING

Finance may be defined as the art and science of managing money. The major areas of finance are Financial Services and Managerial Finance or Financial Management.

Financial Services is concerned with the design and delivery of advice and financial products to individuals, businesses and governments within the areas of banking are related institutions, personal financial planning, investments, real estate, insurance and so on.

Financial Management is concerned with the duties of the financial managers in the business firm.   Financial   managers actively manage the financial affairs of any type of business, namely, financial and non-financial, private and public, large and small, profit seeking and not for profit. They perform such varied tasks as budgeting, financial forecasting, cash management, credit administration, investment analysis, funds management and so on.

Financial Management as an integral part of overall management is not a totally independent area. It   shows   heavily related disciplines and fields of study, such as   economic, accounting, marketing, production and quantitative methods.

9.2   SCOPE OF FINANCIAL MANAGEMENT

Financial management provides a conceptual and analytical framework for financial decision making. Financial management is an integral part of overall management. It covers both financial function of acquisition of funds and allocation of funds. Thus, apart from this involves acquiring the external funds and the main concern of financial management is the efficient and allocation of funds to various uses.

The financial management consider various financial problems of a firm. The main contents of this approach are –

What is the total volume of a firm or enterprise? What

should an enterprise acquire specific assets? How

should the funds required be financed?

It also consider How should be enterprise large and how fast should it grow?

In what form should it hold assets and what is the position of its liabilities.

The financial management covers the major problems of the firm. The main solutions to this problem corresponding under the various decisions taken by the financial managers. Mostly it covers various fields like investment, financing, dividend policy, capital budgeting, working capital management and so on.

9.3   ROLE OF FINANCIAL MANAGEMENT

Role of financial management is very important which are undertaken by finance manager.

1. **In performing financial analysis and planning :** The concern of financial analysis and planning is –

   a. Transforming financial data into a form that can be used to monitor financial condition.

   b. Evaluating the need for increased / reduced productive capacity and

   c. Determining the additional / reduced financing required.

   This activity is fully depend on the financial management. It proves financial management plays on important role in performing financial analysis and planning.

2. **In making investment decisions :** Financial management plays an very important role in making investment decisions like current assets as well as fixed assets. Financial manager must determine and maintain certain optimum level of each assets. He should also decide which of the best fixed asset acquired and when the existing assets need to be modified or replaced or liquidated.

3. **In making financing decisions :** Financial management again plays an vital role in making financing decision. It means the finance manager consider which appropriate mix of short term and long term financing selected and the best individual short term or long term sources of financing at a given point of time. These decisions are dedicated as per necessities, but same require an in-depth analysis of the available financing alternatives, the financial manager considers their costs and their long term implications.

9.4   FUNCTIONAL AREAS OF FINANCIAL MANAGEMENT

Financial management can be broken down into three different functional areas are as follows –

1. The investment decision
2. The financing decision and
3. The dividend policy decision

1. **The Investment Decision :** The investment decision relates to the selection of assets in which the funds will be invested by firm. The assets can be acquired fall into 2 categories :

   i) Long term assets (fixed assets) which yields a return over a period of time.

ii) Short term or current assets defined as those assets which in the normal course of business are convertible into cash without diminution in value usually within a year.

The investment decision policy is also known as capital budgeting management. If the funds are invested in a long term period for acquiring fixed assets is called as capital budgeting management and vice-versa. If the funds are invested in a current assets is popularly for short term period known as working capital management.

2. **Financing Decision** : The second major decision involved in financial management is the financing decision. This is concern with the financing mix or capital structure or leverage. The term capital structure refers to the proportion of debt and equity capital. It means the choice of the proportion of these sources of finance is the capital requirement. It gives the theoretical relationship between the employment of debt and the return to the shareholders.

3. **Dividend policy decision :**The major third decision area of financial management is decision relating to the dividend policy. The dividend decision should be analysed in relation to the financing decision of a firm. The two alternatives are available, i.e. i) The available profits can distributed among the shareholders in the form of dividend or ii) The available profits can be reinvested into business. The decision as to which course should be followed depends largely on a significant element in the dividend decision, the dividend pay our ratio, that is, what proportion of net profits should be paid out to the shareholders.

9.5 VARIOUS FINANCIAL MANAGEMENT TOOLS

Following are various financial management tools:

1. Cash flow statement
2. Fund flow statement
3. Ratio analysis

9.5.1 Cash Flow Statement :

Cash flow statement means a statement of showing net changes in the position of cash and cash equivalents.

As per as 3, this would include cash in hand and savings, current account balances with banks, demand deposits with banks and cash equivalents.

Cash equivalents are defined as short term and highly liquid investments that are readily convertible into cash which are subject to insignificant risk of changes in values.

Uses / advantages of Cash Flow Statement :

1. **Efficient Cash Management :** The most important function of management is to manage the cash resources in such a way that adequate cash is available for meeting the expenses. It helps to plan and co-ordinate the financial operation of the business.

2. **Internal Financial Management :** It provides a clear picture of cash flow operations. Therefore, it is very useful for internal financial management.

3. **Knowledge of changes in Cash Position :** It enables the management to know about the causes of changes in cash position. The finance manager can explain the relationship between profit and cash balance.

4. **Success or failure of Cash Planning :** Cash flow statement helps to management in making the comparison between actual and budgeted cash flow statement to know the success or failure in cash management. It also helps in taking necessary remedial measures in cash of any deviations.

5. **Projected Cash Flow :** It helps to know the projected cash inflow and cash outflow.

6. **Supplemental to Fund Flow Statement :** It is supplementary to Fund flow statement for analysis of cash.

7. **Tool of Analysis :** It analysis is certainly a better tool of analysis than the fund flow analysis for short term decisions.

Limitations of Cash Flow Statement :

1. **Misleading of Inter – Industry Comparison :** Cash flow statement does not measure the economic efficiency of one company in relation to another company. Therefore, due to inter-industry comparison of cash flow may mislead.

2. **Misleading Inter – Firm Comparison :** The terms and conditions of purchases and sales of different firms may not be the same. Hence, inter firm comparison becomes misleading.

3. **Influence of Management Policies :** Management policies influence the cash easily by making certain payments in advance or by postponing certain payments.

4. **Can not tally with Income Statement :** Cash Flow Statement can not be tally with income statement. Therefore, net cash flow does not mean income of the business.

5. **Not a substitute to other statement :** It can not be substitute to other statements. For eg. Fund Flow Statement and Balance Sheet.

9.5.2 Fund Flow Statement :

Fund flow statement shows the sources and uses of funds as well as net change in working capital. It is a financial statement which shows as to how a business entity has obtained its funds and how it has applied or employed its funds between the opening and closing Balance Sheet dates during the particular year or period.

Uses / advantages of Fund Flow Statement :

1. Fund flow statement helps the management in the assessment of long range forecasts of a cash requirements and availability of liquid resources. The manager can judge the quality of management decisions.

2. With the help of Fund Flow Statement, the investors are able to measure as to how the company has utilized the funds supplied by them and its financial strength. Also, the investors can judge the company"s capacity to generate funds from operations.

3. It serves as effective tools to the Management for economic analysis as it supplies additional information which can not be provided by financial statement based on historical data.

4. Fund flow statement explains the relationship between changes in working capital and net profits.

5. Fund flow statement helps the management in making planning process of a company. It is also useful in assessing the resources available and the manner of utilization of the resources.

6. It explains the financial consequences of business activities. It also provides explicit and clean answer to questions regarding liquid and solvency position of the company.

7. Fund Flow Statement provides clues to the creditors and financial institutions as to the ability of a company to use funds effectively in the best interest of the investors, creditors and owners of the company.

Limitations of Fund Flow Statements

1. It should not be overlooked that Fund Statements ignore non- cash transactions, therefore it is considered as cruder device than the financial statement.

2. Fund Flow Statements merely rearrange a part of the information contained in financial statements. They do not serve as original evidence of financial status.

3. Though changes in cash resources are more significant, they are not highlighted by Fund Statements except being shown by them as a part of working capital.

4. As Fund Flow Statements are prepared from information provided by financial statements, they are essentially historical in nature.

Distinction between Cash Flow Statement & Fund Flow Statement

Cash Flow Statement	Fund Flow Statement
It shows net change in the position of cash and cash equivalents	It shows change in the position of „working capital".
It is based on narrower concept of funds i.e. cash and cash equivalents.	It is based on broader concept of funds i.e. working capital.
Now, it is mandatory for all the listed companies and is more widely used in India or abroad.	It is not mandatory and it is not being used by the companies.
Changes in working capital are adjusted for ascertaining cash generated from operations.	Statement of changes in working capital is prepared under fund flow statement.
In Cash flow statement, decrease in current liability or increase in current assets results in decrease in cash and vice – versa.	In working capital, decrease in current liability or increase in current asset brings increase in working capital and vice – versa.

9.5.3 Ratio Analysis:

Financial statement gives us clear idea about the financial position of the company. It will help the proprietor whether to continue the business or closed down or to make changes in working style of the business. Every businessman is interested in profit margin only. Financial statement gives the clear idea of the profit margin in amounting term. But with the help of ratio, we get the clear idea of comparison and with the help of ratio we are able to express the relationship between different figures.

Ratios express the relationship between two number as well as accounting figures. It shows the process of computing and presenting the relationship between items of the financial statement.

The ratio can be expressed in 3 terms:

1. Simple or pure ratio.

2. Percentage.

3. Rate.

9.6   EXERCISE

1. Explain fund flow and cash flow.

2. Distinguish between Fund flow and Cash flow.

3. Define financial management. Briefly explain the functional areas of FM.

4. Explain the tools of Financial Management.

5. Elaborate the role of Financial Management in decision making.

❑❑❑❑❑

Unit - 10
RATIO ANALYSIS

Unit Structure:

10.0 OBJECTIVES

After studying the unit the students will be able to:
- Define Ratio.
- Understand the classification of ratio.
- Know the forms in which the ratios can be expressed. Explain
- the advantages and limitations of ratio analyses.

10.1 INTRODUCTION

Financial statement gives us clear idea about the financial position of the company. It will help the proprietor whether to continue the business or closed down or to make changes in working style of the business. Every businessman is interested in profit margin only. Financial statement gives the clear idea of the profit margin in amounting term. But with the help of ratio, we get the clear idea of comparison and with the help of ratio we are able to express the relationship between different figures.

10.2 MEANING

Ratios express the relationship between two number as well as accounting figures.It   shows   the   process   of   computing   and presentingthe relationship   between items of the financial statement.

145

10.3 FORMS:-

The ratio can be expressed in 3 terms:

1. Simple or pure ratio.
2. Percentage.
3. Rate.

1. Simple or pure ratio -

It gives a simple relationship between two figures. We take simple example of current ratio, it means consider the relationship between current assets and current liabilities, if the current assets are Rs.4,00,000/- and current liabilities are Rs.2,00,000/-, the ratio is derived by dividing Rs.4,00,000/- by Rs.2,00,000/-, then the answer is 2 which will be expressed on 2:1.

2. Percentage -

Some ratio"s is expressed in terms of percentage. The relationship between profit and sales is expressed in percentage. For example- If sales are Rs.10, 00,000/- and gross profit is Rs.5,00,000/- then it is expressed as gross profit being 50% of sales.

3. Rate-

Ratios are also expressed in terms of rates. i.e. number of times or certain period. The relationship between stock is expressed in terms of rates. For Example- If stock turn over rate is said to be 6 times in a year, it mean that the stock is converted into sales 6 times in 12 months.

10.4 CLASSIFICATION

Ratios are classified as follow:

1. Based on financial statement
2. Based on function
3. Based on user

10.4.1 Based on financial statement :

The relationship between two figures which is expressed, it is taken from financial statement i.e. profit and loss a/c, balance sheet or both. This can be grouped as follows.

I. Balance sheet ratio -

The relationship between two figures is expressed by taking figures from balance sheet itself. There is no need to refer income statement. Actually, the relationship between the assets and liabilities is current ratio, liquid ratio, proprietary ratio capital gearing ratio, debt equity ratio, and stock-working capital ratio.

b. Current assets include assets which are circulated and liquidated in cash within one accounting period. E.g. Debtors (net), bills receivables, short term investment, inventories, loose tools etc.

c. Current Liabilities, any liability which is due to be paid within one accounting period is a current liability. E.g. Creditors, bills payable, outstanding expenses, proposed dividend, bank overdraft etc.

d. Significance - It indicates the strength of working capital and measures short term solvency of the business. It reflects the ability of business to pay its short term liabilities.

e. Standard - Normally, 2:1 is regarded as standard ratio which means current assets must be nearly two times of current liabilities.

f. Limitations - It ignores the components of working capital by considering liquid assets and deferred assets as same. It also ignores the quality of working capital by including dead stock in working capital.

g. Example:

Current Assets or a company on Rs. 4,00,000 and on the same data, current liabilities are Rs. 2,00,000. Then

$$\text{Current Ratio} = \frac{\text{Current Assets}}{\text{Current Liabilities}}$$

$$= \frac{4,00,000}{2,00,000}$$

$$= 2:1$$

10.5.3 Quick Ratio / Liquid Ratio / Acid Test Ratio -

Liquid ratio compares the quick assets with the quick liabilities. It is expressed in the form of a pure ratio and it is also known as quick ratio and Acid Ratio.

a. $\text{Quick Ratio} = \dfrac{\text{Quick Assets}}{\text{Quick Liabilities}}$

b. Quick Assets include all current assets minus stock and prepaid expenses.

c. Quick Liabilities includes all current liabilities minus advances received and bank overdraft.

d. Significance - It helps to know the immediate short term liabilities and abilities of business to pay them.

e. Standard - Normally, 1:1 is the standard quick ratio which means quick assets must be at least equal to quick liabilities.

f. Limitation- It may not indicate the long term solvency of the business.

g. Example:

From the following information given calculate 1) Quick Assets 2) Quick Liabilities and 3) Quick Ratio.

Particulars	Amt	Particulars	Amt
Cash	5,000	Outstanding Salaries	1,000
Debtors	10,000	Bank Overdraft	2,000
Creditors	5,000	Stock	3,000
Prepaid Expenses	2,000	Bills Payable	4,000
Bills Receivable	8,000		

Solution:-

Quick Assets:-

Cash	5,000
Debtors	10,000
Bills Receivable	8,000
Total	23,000

Quick Liabilities:-

Creditors	5,000
Outstanding Salary	1,000
Bills Payable	4,000
Total	10,000

$$\text{Quick Ratio} = \frac{\text{Quick Assets}}{\text{Quick Liabilities}}$$

$$= \frac{23,000}{10,000}$$

$$= 2:3:1$$

10.5.4 Stock-Working Capital Ratio -

This ratio shows the relationship between the closing stock and the working capital.

a. $\text{Stock} - \text{Working Capital Ratio} = \dfrac{\text{Stock}}{\text{Working Capital}} \times 100$

b. Stock means closing stock.

152

c. Working capital is equal to current assets minus current liabilities.

d. Significance - It shows the quality of working capital and the quantum of stock in it.

e. Standard - It is practically not possible to have a standard. f.

Example:

If inventory is Rs.80,000/- & Working Capital Rs.1,20,000/- the stock to Working Capital Ratio would be

$$= \frac{Stock}{Working\,Capital} \times$$

$$= \frac{80,000}{1,20,000} \times$$

Stock working capital ratio   =67%

10.5.5 Proprietary Ratio / Net Worth Ratio / Assets Backing Ratio-

It compares proprietor's funds with total liabilities or total assets. It is expressed in terms of percentage.

a. Proprietory Ratio $= \dfrac{Proprietors\,Funds}{Total\,Assets} \times 100$

b. Proprietors funds, includes paid up preference share capital, paid up Equity Share Capital, Capital Reserve, Revenue Reserve, Security Reserve , Profit & Loss Account minus Accumulated losses and fictitious assets.

c. Total Assets includes Fixed Assets, investments and current assets.

d. Significance - It determines to what extent total assets are financed by proprietors. It also compares proprietors funds with total assets and total liabilities. It also indicated as Total Assets = Total Liabilities, Total Liabilities = Proprietors Funds + Loans + Current Liabilities.

e. Standard - It should be very high or very low. Normally, it should be guided as 65%-75% considered. But, it differs from business to business.

f. Example: **Proprietary Ratio -**

From the following information calculate proprietary Ratio or S Ltd.

Particulars	Amt
Equity share capital	1,50,000
Preference share capital	50,000
Reserves	30,000
Proprietors funds	2,30,000
Current Assets	1,00,000
Fixed Assets	2,50,000
Total Assets	3,50,000

$$\text{Proprietory Ratio} = \frac{\text{Proprietors Fund}}{\text{Total Assets}} \times 100$$

$$= \frac{23,000}{35,000} \times$$

$$= 66\%$$

10.5.6 Debt Equity Ratio -

This ratio compares the long term debts with shareholders" funds. It is usually expressed as a pure ratio.

a. $\text{Debt Equity Ratio} = \dfrac{\text{Debt}}{\text{Equity}}$

OR

$$\frac{\text{Loan Funds}}{\text{Owned Funds}}$$

b. Debt includes borrowed funds as secured / Unsecured loans including debentures, interest accrues and due on loans.

c. Proprietors funds includes paid up share capital, Reserves and surplus minus fictitious assets and accumulated losses.

d. Significance - This is a solvency ratio and it also indicated the proportion of debt and equity in financing the funds of the concerns. It also shows protection cover for long term creditors. The low debt equity ratio is considered as favourable to creditors. It indicates, low ratio means less dependence on long term debts.

e. Standard - If debts equity ratio is two third then it is considered as satisfactory ratio. It implies that out of three total funds debts would be 2 and Equity would be 1.

f. Example: **Debt Equity Ratio -**

From the following information calculate Debt - Equity Ratio or P Ltd.

Particulars	Amt
5 % Debentures	4,00,000
7 % Preference share Capital	2,00,000
Equity Capital	3,00,000

$$\text{Debt Equity Ratio} = \frac{\text{Borrowed funds}}{\text{Funds}}$$

$$= \frac{4,00,000}{5,00,000}$$

$$= 0.8$$

10.5.7 Capital Gearing Ratio / Financing Leverage Ratio / Capital Structure Ratio -

Gearing means the process of increasing the equity shareholders" return through the use of debt. Equity shareholders earn more when the rate or return on total capital is more than the rate of interest on debts.

a. Capital Gearing Ratio $= \dfrac{\text{Capital Bearing Fixed Rate of Interest \& Dividend}}{\text{Capital Not Bearing Fixed Rate of Interest \& Dividend.}}$

b. Capital bearing fixed rate of interest and dividend includes Preference share capital, debentures, loans etc.

c. Capital not bearing fixed rate of interest and dividend includes equity share capital, reserves and surplus, fictitious assets and accumulated losses.

d. Significance - It shows balance between debt and equity and it also shows whether a company is practicing trading on equity.

e. Example: **Capital Gearing Ratio-**

The following are the relevant extract from Balance sheet or ABC Ltd as on 31st Dec, 2003. Calculate the capital gearing ratio.

Liabilities	Amt
8,000 Equity share or Rs.10/- each Fully Paid	80,000
9% Preference Shares or Rs.100/- cash fully paid	1,50,000
Security (share) Premium	10,000
Capital Reserve	16,000
10% Debentures	50,000

$$\text{Capital Gearing Ratio} = \frac{\text{Capital entitled to fixed Interest / Dividend}}{\text{Capital not entitled to fixed Interest / Dividend}}$$

OR

$$= \frac{\text{Preference Capital} + \text{Debentures}}{\text{Equity Capital} + \text{Share Premium} + \text{Capital Reserve}}$$

$$= \frac{1,50,000 + 50,000}{80,000 + 10,000 + 16,000}$$

$$= \frac{2,00,000}{1,06,000}$$

$$= 1.89$$

10.6 REVENUE STATEMENT RATIO

10.6.1 Format of Revenue statement

Profit & Loss A/c.
Vertical Income / Revenue Statement

Particulars	Amt	Amt	Amt
Credit Sales Cash		XX	
Sales Total Sales		XX	
Opening Stock			XX
Credit Purchases		XX	
Cash Purchases	XX		
Total Purchases	XX		
Direct Expenses		XX	
(-) Closing Stock Cost		XX	
of Good Sold Gross		(XX)	
Profit Operating Exp			(XX)
Administrative Exp			XX
Selling Expenses			
Finance Exp (Excl. Interest)		XX	
Operating Profit		XX	
(+) Non Operating Income		XX	(XX)
			XX
(-) Non Operating Exp			XX
Profit Before Interest & Tax			(XX)
(-) Interest on loans			XX
			(XX)
Net Profit Before Tax			XX
(-) Income Tax			(XX)
Net Profit after Tax			XX
(-) Preference Dividend			(XX)
Profit available for Equity Shareholders			XX
(-) Equity Dividend			(XX)
Retained Earning			XX

10.6.2 Gross Profit Ratio -

This ratio compares gross profit with net sales.

a. $\text{Gross Profit Ratio} = \dfrac{\text{Gross Profit}}{\text{Net Sales}} \times 100$

b. Gross Profit = Sales minus Cost of Goods Sold

   (Cost of Goods Sold = Opening Stock + Purchases + Direct Expense - Closing Stock)

c. Net Sales = Sales minus Sales Returns minus Allowances.

d. Significance - It indicates basic profitability of business concern, it also indicate the efficiency of the purchase department, production department and the sales department. It shows the percentage of mark up on the goods sold.

e. Example: **Gross Profit Ratio -**

Net Sales	Rs. 5,00,000
(-) Cost of Goods Sold	Rs. 4,20,000
Gross Profit	80,000

Calculate Gross Profit Ratio.

$$\text{Gross Profit Ratio} = \frac{\text{Gross Profit}}{\text{Sales}} \times$$

$$= \frac{80,000}{5,00,000} \times 100$$

$$= 16\%$$

10.6.3 Operating Ratio –

It expresses the relationship between total operating costs and net sales.

a) Operating Ratio $= \dfrac{\text{Operating Cost}}{\text{Net Sales}} \times 100$

$= \dfrac{\text{cost of goods sold} + \text{Operating Expenses}}{\text{Net Sales}} \times 100$

b) It expresses the relationship between each item of expenditure with sales. It brings out the relationship between elements of operating cost and net sales.

c) Significance - This enables the management in controlling cost and improving profit ability as well as the auditor and income tax department to judge the correctness and reliability of various expenses.

d) Limitations - If expenses of fixed amount the ratio of expenses to sales may be increased or decreased in value. The ratio of variable expenses may remain same even though sales are increased.

e) Example: **Operating Ratio -**

Calculate operating ratio from the following information.

Sales	Rs. 20,00,000
Gross Profit	Rs. 7,00,000
Operating Expenses	Rs. 5,00,000

Cost of goods sold = Sales less Gross Profit

1,30,000 = 20,00,000 - 7,00,000

Operating Ratio $= \dfrac{\text{Cost of Goods Sold} + \text{Operating expenses}}{\text{Net Sales}} \times 100$

$= \dfrac{13,00,000 + 5,00,000}{20,00,000} \times 100$

$= 90\%$

Calculate various expenses ratios and operating ratio from the following information.

i) Cost of goods sold	Rs.	40,000
ii) Office & Administrative expenses	Rs.	20,000
iii) Selling & distribution Expenses	Rs.	15,000
iv) Sales	Rs.	1,00,000

i) Cost of goods sold Ratio $= \dfrac{\text{cost of goods sold}}{\text{Sales}} \times 100$

$$= \frac{40,000}{10,000} \times 100$$

$$= 40\%$$

ii) Office & administrative Expenses Ratio

$$= \frac{\text{Office \& Administrative Expenses}}{\text{Sales}} \times 100$$

$$= \frac{20,000}{1,00,000} \times 100$$

$$= 20\%$$

iii) Selling & distribution Expenses Ratio

$$= \frac{\text{Selling \& distribution Expenses}}{\text{Sales}} \times 100$$

$$= \frac{15,000}{1,00,000} \times 100$$

$$= 15\%$$

iv) Operating Ratio $= \dfrac{\text{Cost of goods sold} + \text{Operating Exp}}{\text{Net Sales}} \times 100$

$$= \frac{40,000 + 20,000 + 15,000}{1,00,000} \times 100$$

$$= 75\%$$

10.6.4 Net Profit Ratio -

Net profit ratio indicates the relationship between net profit and the sales. It is usually expressed in the form of a percentage.

a) It is calculated in three ways.

i. Net Operating Profit Ratio $= \dfrac{\text{Net Operating Profit}}{\text{Net Sales}} \times 100$

ii. Net Profit Ratio $= \dfrac{\text{Net Profit before tax}}{\text{Net Sales}} \times 100$

iii. Net Profit Ratio $= \dfrac{\text{Net Profit after tax}}{\text{Net Sales}} \times 100$

b) Net Profit before tax = Operating Net profit + Non operating income - Non operating expenses.

Net profit after tax = Net profit before tax - income tax

c) Net Sales = Gross sales minus Returns minus allowances

d) Significance - It indicates overall profitability of business organization, it also indicates as to what portion of net profit is available to the proprietors.

e) Limitations - It cannot be used as a text Net profit Ratio without considering other revenue statement ratio. It may be also affected by non operating income of expenses, income from extra ordinary transaction. In such cases, Net profit ratio may be showing higher or lower volume even though sales and other cost may be showing the same tendency as before and hence net profit Ratio is isolation cannot provide clear idea about the company"s profitability.

f) Example: **Net Profit Ratio -**

Calculate Net Profit Ratio from the following :

Operating Net Profit	Rs.1,50,000
Non Operating Income	Rs.25,000
Non Operating Expenses	Rs.20,000
Net Sales	Rs.10,00,000

$$\text{Net Profit Ratio} = \frac{\text{Net Profit before Tax}}{\text{Sales}} \times 100$$

NPBT = Operating Net Profit + Non Operating Income - Non Operating Expenses

$$= 1,50,000 + 25,000 - 20,000$$

$$= 1,55,000$$

$$\text{NP Ratio} = \frac{1,55,000}{10,00,000} \times 100$$

$$= 15.5\%$$

10.6.5 Stock Turnover Ratio / Stock velocity Ratio / inventory Turnover Ratio -

Stock turnover ratio shows the relationship between the cost of goods sold and the average stock.

a) $$\text{Stock turnover Ratio} = \frac{\text{cost of goods sold}}{\text{Average stock}}$$

OR

$$= \frac{\text{Net Sales}}{\text{Average stock at selling price}}$$

b) Cost of goods sold = Opening stock + Purchases + Direct expenses - closing stock

c) Average stock $= \dfrac{\text{Opening stock } + \text{ closing Stock}}{2}$

d) Significance - Stock turnover ratio helps in determining the frequency of inventory replacement. It also helps in determining the liquidity of business organization.

e) Limitations - It should be studied along with current ratio stock working capital ratio. Stock being differed from current assets, current ratio may be satisfactory due to large stock, but it may suffer bud quick ratio.

f) Example: **Stock Turnover Ratio -**

If cost of sales is Rs.25,00,000/- and opening stock Rs.3,00,000/- and closing stock Rs.2,00,000/-. Calculate Stock Turnover Ratio.

$$\text{Average Stock} = \dfrac{\text{Opening Stock } + \text{ Closing Stock}}{2}$$

$$= \dfrac{3,00,000 + 2,00,000}{2}$$

$$= 2,50,000$$

$$\text{Stock Turnover Ratio} = \dfrac{\text{Cost of Sales}}{\text{Average Stock}}$$

$$= \dfrac{25,00,000}{2,50,000}$$

$$= 10 \text{ times}$$

10.6.6 Operating Profit Ratio -

Operating profit ratio indicates the relationship between Operating profit and Sales.

a) Operating Profit Ratio $= \dfrac{\text{Operating Profit}}{\text{Net Sales}} \times 100$

b) Operating profit = Gross profit minus operating expenses, •

Operating expenses =

    1   Office and administrative expenses

    2   Selling a distribution expenses

> 3 Finance expenses excluding interest on loans and Debentures.

c) Net Sales = Sales less Returns less Allowances.

d) Significance - It is a profitability ratio, which shows the relationship between profits and sales, it also indicates profits from operations.

e) Example: **Operating Profit Ratio -**

Calculate operating net profit ratio from the following data.

Gross Profit	Rs.4,00,000
Office Expenses	Rs.1,50,000
Selling Expenses	Rs.1,00,000
Sales	Rs.10,00,000

Operating Net Profit = Gross Profit less Selling Expenses less Office Expenses

1,50,000 = 4,00,000 - 1,00,000 - 1,50,000

$$\text{Operating Net Profit Ratio} = \frac{\text{Operating Net Profit}}{\text{Net Sales}} \times 100$$

$$= \frac{1,50,000}{10,00,000} \times 100$$

$$= 15\%$$

10.7 COMPOSITE RATIO

10.7.1 Return on capital employed -

This ratio measures the relationship between net profit (before interest & tax) and the capital employed to earn it. It is expressed as a percentage.

$$\text{a) Return on capital employed} = \frac{\text{Net profit before interest, Tax, dividend}}{\text{Capital employed}} \times 100$$

b) Net Profit before interest, tax and dividend

c) Capital Employed = Proprietors fund + Long Term Loans

OR

Fixed Assets + Current Assets - current liabilities.

d) Significance - It gives clear index or utilization of assets earning capacity. This ratio measures the overall profitability from the total funds employed. It means, measures the relationship between net profit before interest, tax and capital employed to earn net profit.

e) Limitations - This ratio is based on earning and capital employed of the business. These components are subject to various manipulations by management or based on various different accounting policies.

f) Example: **Return On Capital Employed** -

Calculate return on capital employed from the following data. Net

Profit   Rs.   2,00,000

Capital Employed   Rs. 20,00,000

$$\text{Return on Capital Employed} = \frac{\text{Net Profit}}{\text{Capital Employed}} \times 100$$

$$= \frac{2,00,000}{20,00,000} \times 100$$

$$= 10\%$$

1.7.2 Return on proprietors fund / Return on proprietors Equity -

It measures the relationship between profits available to proprietor funds.

a) $\text{Return on proprietors fund} = \dfrac{\text{Net profit after Tax}}{\text{proprietors fund}} \times 100$

b) Net profit after Tax

c) Proprietors funds includes paid up Preference share capital, paid up equity share capital, capital Reserve, Revenue Reserve, Security Reserve, Profit and Loss A/C surplus minus Accumulated losses and fictitious Assets.

d) Significance - Higher ratio signifies better utilization of funds. It also measures the overall performance of a business in regards utilization of total resources available.

e) Example: **Return on Proprietors fund-**

The following is the relevant extract from the Profit & Loss A/c & Balance Sheet of SR Ltd. as on 31. 03. 2004

Profit & Loss A/c, for the year ended 31. 03. 04

Dr.   Cr.

Particulars	Amt	Particulars	Amt
To Administrative Exp.	80,000	By Gross Profit b/d	2,00,000
To Selling Expenses	30,000		
To Provision for Tax	20,000		
To Net Profit c/d	70,000		
	2,00,000		2,00,000

Balance Sheet as on 31. 03. 2004

Particulars	Amt	Amt
Share Capital		
600, 7% Preference Shares of Rs.100/- each fully paid	60,000	
1,500, Equity Shares of Rs.100/- each fully paid	1,50,000	2,10,000
Reserves		
General Reserve	40,000	
Capital Redemption Reserve	30,000	
Dividend Equalisation Fund	20,000	90,000
		3,00,000

10.7.3 Return on Equity Share Capital –

It indicates the rate of earning on equity share capital.

a) Return on Equity Share Capital $= \dfrac{\text{Net Profit after Tax } - \text{ Preference Dividend}}{\text{Share Capital}} \times 100$

b) Net Profit after Tax minus Preference dividend.

c) Equity Share Capital includes paid up equity share capital.

d) Significance - It includes an investor in shares of company whether continue to hold or dispose off such shares.   It also enables investors to compare earnings of the company with that another company.   Higher ratio signifies better utilization of shareholders fund and higher return on equity share capital.

e) Example: **Return on Equity Share Capital -**

From the following information calculate Return on Equity Capital Ratio.

Net Profit after Tax	3,25,000
7% Preference share capital	1,50,000
Paid up Equity share capital	10,00,000

$$\text{Return on Equity Capital} = \dfrac{\text{Net Profit less Preference dividend}}{\text{Paidup Equity Capital}}$$

$$= \dfrac{3,25,000 - (7\% \text{ of } 1,50,000)}{10,00,000} \times 100$$

$$= \dfrac{3,25,000 - 10,500}{10,00,000} \times 100$$

$$= \dfrac{3,14,500}{10,00,000} \times 100$$

$$= 31.45\%$$

10.7.4 Earning Per Share -

It shows earning per equity share, whether or not company declares dividend.

a) Earning per share $= \dfrac{\text{Net Profit after Tax} - \text{Preference Dividend}}{\text{Number of Equity Shares}}$

b) Net profit after Tax minus Preference dividend. c)

Number of equity shares outstanding.

$$= \underline{\qquad\qquad\qquad\qquad\qquad\qquad} \times$$

d) Significance - Higher ratio signifies better utilization of funds available and the company may pay dividend at a higher rate in future. Higher ratio indicates higher overall profitability and effective utilization of equity capital.

e) Example: **Earning Per Share-**

Net Profit after Tax	Rs.2,25,000
8% Preference Share Capital	Rs.2,00,000
Paid up Equity Share Capital	Rs.10,00,000
(Rs. 100/- each)	

Earning Per Share $= \dfrac{\text{Net Profit after Tax} - \text{Preference dividend}}{\text{No. of Equity Share}}$

$$\text{No. of Equity Shares} = \frac{\text{Share Capital}}{\text{Face Value Per Share}}$$

$$= \frac{10,00,000}{100}$$

$$= 10,000 \text{ Shares}$$

$$= \frac{2,25,000 - (8\% \text{ of } 2,00,000)}{10,000}$$

$$= \frac{2,25,000 - 16,000}{10,000}$$

$$= \frac{2,09,000}{10,000}$$

$$= \text{Rs. } 20.90$$

10.7.5 Dividend Payout Ratio -

It shows the relationship between the dividend paid to equity shareholders out of the profits available to equity shareholders.

a) $$\text{Dividend Payout Ratio} = \frac{\text{Dividend Per Equity Share}}{\text{Earning per Share}}$$

b) Dividend per share equity share means dividend paid on one equity share.

c) Earning per share is calculated as per above formula.

d) Significance - It measures dividend paying capacity of the company. Higher ratio signifies the company has utilized larger portion of its earning for payment of dividend. Low ratio indicates that smaller portion of earning has been utilized for payment of dividend. It also indicated that larger portion of earnings had been retained.

e) Example: **Dividend Payout Ratio -**

Net Profit after Tax	Rs.	3,25,000
7% Preference Share Capital	Rs.	2,00,000
Paid up Equity share		
Capital of Rs. 10 per share	Rs.	10,00,000
Equity Dividend @ Rs. 1 per share		

$$\text{Dividend Payout Ratio} = \frac{\text{Dividend to Equity Shareholders}}{\text{Profit available to Equity shareholders}} \times 100$$

$$= \frac{10,00,000}{3,25,000 - 14,000} \times 100$$

$$= \frac{10,00,000}{3,25,000 \ (7\% \ of \ 2,00,000)} \times 100$$

$$= \frac{10,00,000}{3,11,000} \times 100$$

$$= 32.15\%$$

10.7.6 Dividend Yield Ratio -

It shows the relationship between dividend per share earned by shareholder on market price of each share.

a) $\text{Dividend Yield Ratio} = \dfrac{\text{Dividend Per Share}}{\text{Market Price per share}}$

b) Dividend per share is derived by dividing Total Dividend payout to Number of Shares.

c) Market price per share is the quotation price in the stock market. d)

Significance - This ratio indicates the ultimate current return which investors will get as a percentage on its current market value of shares. It also indicates dividend policy of the company.

e) Example: **Dividend Yield Ratio** -

Dividend per Share	Rs.10
Market Price per Share	Rs.100

$$\text{Dividend Yield Ratio} = \frac{\text{Dividend Per Share}}{\text{Market Price Per Share}}$$

$$= \frac{10}{100} \times 100$$

$$= 10\%$$

10.7.7 Price Earnings Ratio -

It brings out the relationship between market price per share with earning per share.

a) Price Earning Ratio $= \dfrac{\text{Market Price Per share}}{\text{Earning per Share}}$

b) Market price of one share is value of one share in the market. c)

Earning per share.

d) Significance - It indicates the relationship between market price of share and current earning per share. It also helps in determining the future value of the share.

e) Example: **Price Earnings Ratio -**

Net Profit after Tax	Rs.3,25,000
7% Preference Share Capital	Rs.2,00,000
Paid up Equity Share	
Capital of Rs. 100 per share	Rs.10,00,000
Market Price per share	Rs.210/-

Earning Per Share $= \dfrac{\text{Net Profit ater Tax} - \text{Preference dividend}}{\text{No. of Equity Shares}}$

No. of Equity Shares $= \dfrac{\text{Equity Share Capital}}{\text{Face Value Per Share}}$

Price Earning Ratio $= \dfrac{\text{Market Price Per Share}}{\text{Earning Per Share}}$

No. of Equity Shares $= \dfrac{10,00,000}{100} = 10,000 \text{ Shares}$

EPS $= \dfrac{3,25,000 - 14,000}{10,000} = 31.10$

PER $= \dfrac{210}{31.10} = 6.75$

10.7.8 Fixed Assets Turnover Ratio –

It indicates the frequency of fixed assets utilization.

a) Fixed Assets Turnover Ratio $= \dfrac{\text{Net Assets}}{\text{Fixed Assets}}$

b) Net Sales = Gross Sales minus Sales Return minus Allowances.

c) Fixed Assets includes assets acquired for long term use in the business and not for sale in ordinary course of business. For e.g. Goodwill, Land & Building, Plant & Machinery, Vehicles etc.

d) Significance - It indicates efficiency in or extend of utilization of fixed assets. Higher ratio indicates high degree of efficiency in utilization and low degree signifies vice-versa.

e) Example: **Fixed Assets Turnover Ratio -**

If sales are Rs.10,00,000/- and Fixed Assets are Rs.3,00,000/- calculate Fixed Assets.

$$\text{Turnover Ratio} \quad = \quad \frac{\text{Net Sales}}{\text{Fixed Assets}} \quad = \quad \frac{1,00,000}{3,00,000} \quad =$$

10.7.9 Total Assets Turnover Ratio -

It shows the relationship between net sales and total assets.

a) Total Assets Turnover Ratio $\quad = \quad \dfrac{\text{Net Sales}}{\text{Total Assets}}$

b) Net Sales = Gross sales minus Returns minus Allowances.

c) Total Fixed Assets = Fixed Assets + Investment + Current Assets but excluding fictitious assets.

d) Significance - It indicates how efficiency assets are employed overall.

e) Example: **Total Assets Turnover Ratio -**

Total Assets = Fixed Assets + Current Assets
  5,00,000   =   3,00,000   +   2,00,000

Turnover Rs.10,00,000/-

$$\text{Total Assets Turnover Ratio} \quad = \quad \frac{\text{Net Sales}}{\text{Total Assets}}$$

$$= \quad \frac{10,00,000}{5,00,000}$$

$$= 20$$

10.7.10 Debt Service Ratio / Interest Coverage Ratio -

This ratio shows the relationship between earning before interest and interest on long term loans. The main purpose of this ratio is to find out the number of times the fixed interest charges are covered by the income before interest and tax.

a) Debt Service Ratio $= \dfrac{\text{Net Profit before Interest \& Tax}}{\text{Fixed Interest Charges}}$

b) Profit before interest & tax means the amount of net profit before interest and tax. Interest means the interest payable on loans.

c) Fixed interest charges mean interest on long term loans.

d) Significance - Its main purposed is to measure the interest paying capacity of the company.

e) Example: **Debt Service Ratio -**

Find out the Debt Service Ratio from the following details a)

Profit before interest and tax Rs.1,00,000/-

b) Interest payable Rs.25,000/-

$$\text{Debt Service Ratio} = \dfrac{\text{Profit before Interest \& Tax}}{\text{Interest}}$$

$$= \dfrac{1,00,000}{25,000}$$

$$= 4$$

10.7.11 Debt Service Coverage Ratio -

It shows the relationship between net profits and interest plus installments payable on loans. It is expressed as a pure number.

a) Debt Service Coverage Ratio $= \dfrac{\text{Cash Profits available for debt servicing}}{\text{Interest} + \text{Installment due on loans}}$

b) Cash profits available for debt servicing are calculated as follows:

  i) Net Profit after interest and Tax

  ii) (+) Non cash debits to Profit & Loss A/c

    (E.g. Depreciation, goodwill w/off, loss on sales of Fixed Assets etc)

iii) Cash Profits for debt servicing.

c) Interest means interest on long term loans during the year.

Installment means installments due on long term loans during the year.

d) Significance - This ratio indicates the company"s ability to pay interest and principal amount on time as it indicates whether company is able to pay interest and repayment of loan out of earnings of the company. It is more useful for lender as it takes care of total repayment liability.

e) Example: **Debt Service Coverage Ratio**

Find out the Debt Service Coverage Ratio from the following details.

1) Profit after interest and tax Rs.2,50,000/-

2) Interest Payable Rs.25,000/-

3) Depreciation Rs.15,000/-

4) Loan installment payable during the year Rs.1,45,000/-.

$$\text{Debt Equity Ratio} = \frac{\text{Net Profit before Interest \& Tax}}{\text{Fixed Interest Charges}}$$

$$= \frac{2,50,000 + 15,000 + 25,000}{25,000 + 1,45,000}$$

$$= 1.70$$

10.7.12 Debtors Turnover Ratio / Debtors Velocity / Accounts Receivable Turnover -

This shows the relationship between net credit sales and average trade debtors. It is expressed as a rate.

$$\text{a) Debtors Turnover Ratio} = \frac{\text{Net Credit Sales}}{\text{Debtors + Bills Receivables}}$$

$$\text{OR}$$

$$\frac{\text{Credit Sales}}{\text{Average Account Receivable}}$$

b) Net Credit Sales = Gross Credit Sales minus Sales Returns

c) Debtors and bills receivable may be taken at the average of opening and closing amounts. If the details are not available only the closing balance may be considered.

d) Example: **Debtors Turnover Ratio -**

From the following information calculate the Debtors Turnover Ratio -

Net Credit Sales	7,30,000
Net Debtors	75,000
Net Bills Receivable	25,000

$$\text{Debtors Turnover Ratio} = \frac{\text{Credit Sales}}{\text{Debtors } + \text{Bills Receivable}}$$

$$= \frac{7,30,000}{1,00,000}$$

$$= 7.3 \text{ times}$$

10.7.13 Creditors Turnover Ratio –

This shows the relationship between the net credit purchases and the average trade creditors. This ratio is normally expressed as a "rate".

$$\text{a) Creditor Turnover Ratio} = \frac{\text{Credit Purchases}}{\text{Average Accounts Payable}}$$

OR

$$\frac{\text{Credit Purchases}}{\text{Creditors } + \text{ Bills Payable}}$$

b) Net Credit Purchases = Gross Credit Purchases - Purchase Return - Allowances on Credit Purchases

c) Creditors and bills payable may be taken at the average of the opening and closing amount. If the details are not available, only the closing balance may be considered.

d) Example: **Credit turnover ratio.**

From the following information calculate the credit turnover ratio.

Net Credit Purchases	Rs.	1,00,000
Creditors	Rs.	20,000
Bills Payable	Rs.	5,000

$$\text{Creditor Turnover} = \frac{\text{Credit Purchases}}{\text{Creditors} + \text{BillsPayable}}$$

$$= \frac{1,00,000}{20,000 + 5,000}$$

$$= \frac{1,00,000}{25,000}$$

$$= 4 \text{ times}$$

10.7.14 Debt Collection Period –

This ratio gives average debt collection period and indicates the extend to each the debts have being collected in time.

a) $\text{Debt Collection Period} = \dfrac{\text{Number of days or months in a year}}{\text{Debtors Turnover Ratio}}$

b) Significance - It indicates credit and collection policy and it also indicates effectiveness of collection from debtors.

c) Example: **Debt Collection Period -**

Debt collection period is calculated from above illustration of the point **10.7.12**

$$\text{Debt Collection Period} = \frac{365}{\text{Debtors Turnover Ratio}}$$

$$= \frac{365}{7.33}$$

$$= 50 \text{ days.}$$

10.7.15 Creditors Payout Ratio -

This shows the relationship between Number of days or months in a year with the promptness in payment of credit purchases.

a) $\text{Creditor Payout Ratio} = \dfrac{\text{No. of day sin a year}}{\text{Creditor Turnover Ratio}}$

b) Significance - It should be compared with actual credit available from suppliers and whether the company is taking full benefit of the credit period allowed by creditors.

c) Example: **Credit Collection Period -**

It is calculated from above illustration No. 10.7.13

$$\text{Credit Collection Period} = \frac{365}{\text{Creditors Turnover Ratio}}$$

$$= \frac{365}{4}$$

$$= \frac{12}{4} \quad 91 \text{ days or 3 months.}$$

10.8 ADVANTAGES AND LIMITATIONS OF RATIO ANALYSIS

10.8.1 Advantages of Ratios Analysis:

Ratio analysis is an important and age-old technique of financial analysis. The following are some of the advantages / Benefits of ratio analysis:

1. **Simplifies financial statements:** It simplifies the comprehension of financial statements. Ratios tell the whole story of changes in the financial condition of the business

2. **Facilitates inter-firm comparison:** It provides data for inter- firm comparison. Ratios highlight the factors associated with with successful and unsuccessful firm. They also reveal strong firms and weak firms, overvalued and undervalued firms.

3. **Helps in planning:** It helps in planning and forecasting. Ratios can assist management, in its basic functions of forecasting. Planning, co-ordination, control and communications.

4. **Makes inter-firm comparison possible:** Ratios analysis also makes possible comparison of the performance of different divisions of the firm. The ratios are helpful in deciding about their efficiency or otherwise in the past and likely performance in the future.

5. **Help in investment decisions:** It helps in investment decisions in the case of investors and lending decisions in the case of bankers etc.

10.8.2 Limitations of Ratios Analysis:

The ratios analysis is one of the most powerful tools of financial management. Though ratios are simple to calculate and easy to understand, they suffer from serious limitations.

1. **Limitations of financial statements:** Ratios are based only on the information which has been recorded in the financial statements. Financial statements themselves are subject to several limitations. Thus ratios derived, there from, are also subject to those limitations. For example, non-financial changes though important for the business are not relevant by the financial statements. Financial statements are affected to a very great extent by accounting conventions and concepts. Personal judgment plays a great part in determining the figures for financial statements.

2. **Comparative study required:** Ratios are useful in judging the efficiency of the business only when they are compared with past results of the business. However, such a comparison only provide glimpse of the past performance and forecasts for future may not prove correct since several other factors like market conditions, management policies, etc. may affect the future operations.

3. **Ratios alone are not adequate:** Ratios are only indicators, they cannot be taken as final regarding good or bad financial position of the business. Other things have also to be seen.

4. **Problems of price level changes:** A change in price level can affect the validity of ratios calculated for different time periods. In such a case the ratio analysis may not clearly indicate the trend in solvency and profitability of the company. The financial statements, therefore, be adjusted keeping in view the price level changes if a meaningful comparison is to be made through accounting ratios.

5. **Lack of adequate standard:** No fixed standard can be laid down for ideal ratios. There are no well accepted standards or rule of thumb for all ratios which can be accepted as norm. It renders interpretation of the ratios difficult.

6. **Limited use of single ratios:** A single ratio, usually, does not convey much of a sense. To make a better interpretation, a number of ratios have to be calculated which is likely to confuse the analyst than help him in making any good decision.

7. **Personal bias:** Ratios are only means of financial analysis and not an end in itself. Ratios have to interpreted and different people may interpret the same ratio in different way.

8. **Incomparable:** Not only industries differ in their nature, but also the firms of the similar business widely differ in their size and accounting procedures etc. It makes comparison of ratios difficult and misleading.

10.9 EXERCISE

1. Explain the advantages and limitations of ratio analyses.
2. Briefly explain the classification of Ratios.
3. Give significance of Following

    Ratios:

- Proprietors ratio
- Debt Equity ratio
- Gross profit ratio
- Stock turnover ratio
- Earnings per share
- Creditors payout ratio

4. Give formula of the ratio:

    - Current Assets • Quick liabilities • Proprietors fund • Capital

    gearing ratio • Net profit before tax • Capital employed • Total Assets

****